Harley James & the Mystery of the Mayan Kings

Leah Cupps

VISION FORTY

Dear Friend,

Welcome! My name is Harley James and this is my story, the Mystery of the Mayan Kings. I'm so glad you're here!

If you love riddles and puzzles as much as I do, then you must download the free activity kit I made, just for you! It includes mazes, puzzles and of course, secret messages!

Go to HarleyJamesAdventures.com to download this fun activity kit for free!

Until then, Happy Reading!

Harley James

P.S. Some of the characters & history in this story is fictional, and some is true. Want to know what's what?

Go to HarleyJamesAdventures.com and click on our free Fact or Fiction Video Series to find out more.

www.HarleyJamesAdventures.com

Dedicated to my daughter, Savannah Cupps.

Her curiosity, adventurous spirit and love of dogs inspired this book.

CONTENTS

PROLOGUE

round 1600 Years Ago in Tikal, Guatemala

Eloy tucked the statue under his arm, tightening his grip as he stumbled forward into the jungle. He could hear the cries of the battle for Tikal behind him and feel the heat from the buildings burning under the pale moon. The statue was vibrating against his bare skin, the green glow around it beating to its own rhythm.

Three thoughts tumbled through his mind...

It was the final night of the 400-year Baktun cycle.

The Three Kings, Jasaw, Yax K'uk, and Jacinto, were dethroned.

The last of their loyalists were being exiled.

Earlier that night, the elders told him that when the Three Kings were defeated, a powerful magic had captured their souls. The priests then cast a spell and locked those souls inside three jade statues.

Separated, the statues were useless stone relics.

But together?

If the statues were reunited on the Eve of the thirteenth Baktun, the Three Kings would return. And in their revenge, they would bring an army of the dead to rule the world.

Eloy, a clever young boy of just eleven years old, had been charged with hiding one of the magical statues. He shuddered for a moment, thinking of what was hidden inside. The statue glowed in his arms, and he felt his feet move a bit quicker, knowing that the cover of night wouldn't last for long.

"Run," his mother had warned him. Her eyes had been bright with fear, her voice quaking as she spoke. She brushed a tuft of black hair from his eyes. "Run, my son, and don't look back."

"I will, Mama," he replied. He willed his knees to stop shaking as he spoke. His mama must not know he was scared.

And now he ran. The elders had told him of an ancient temple hidden in the jungle just a few miles from Tikal. Older than the Temple of the Jaguar. There he would hide the cursed little statue; hidden forever inside, and perhaps he along with it.

He volunteered to make this sacrifice. For the liberation of Tikal. For the protection of the world from the wickedness of the Three Kings.

Shouts emerged from behind him. He pushed his legs harder. His lungs burned as hot as the city in flames behind him.

The loyalists were gaining on him.

When he saw what was just ahead of him, he smiled. They were too late. The temple was just a few more steps away. And once he was inside, the statue would be hidden forever.

In a place where no one would ever find it. Unless, of course, they were good at solving riddles.

CHAPTER 1
THE GLOWING STATUE

*T*ikal, *Guatemala, Present Day*

You know how you just *know* something in your "knower"? As if you had a crystal ball built into your brain?

Well, today I had a feeling. This was going to be my year.

I, Harley Rebecca James, am going to win the Junior International Cryptography Competition.

What is that, you ask?

JICC is an online competition that follows the story of two explorers as they embark on a cryptographic adventure. Solving riddles and clues are my favorite things to do, so naturally, I love cryptography. Each week for twelve weeks, a new chapter is released, with a new code to break. Thousands of kids enter to win. And I was about to solve the clue for week two.

Thirty-nine characters. A famous phrase... got it!

I scribbled the answer down in my journal and smiled.

"Where there is ruin, there is hope for treasure," I whispered to myself.

A quote from the ancient philosopher Rumi. Of course, I've heard Dad say this a hundred times.

The code itself had been easy to crack. The technique used was a simple Caesar shift. The hard part had been finding the key to unlock the cipher.

I couldn't wait to get back to my room so I could log on and enter the answer.

"Harley? Have you finished your report on Mayan glyphs yet?" A voice suddenly broke through my thoughts.

Report?

Right, I was supposed to be finishing my homework, not cracking codes.

"Almost," I replied, tucking a piece of unruly blonde hair out of my face. I was with my tutor Jessica Rodríguez and her dog, Daisy, sitting under the shade of the famous temples of Tikal, an ancient Mayan site nestled in the dense Guatemalan forest.

"Are you solving riddles again?"

I smiled in response, shrugging my shoulders.

"You need to finish your history assignment."

Jessica frowned at me and readjusted her long legs, shifting in her chair. She was pretty when she smiled, but most of the time, I felt like she was scowling at me. I sat upright and grabbed my notebook.

She hated when I got distracted during homework time.

Upon hearing my voice, Daisy rose up from her spot next to Jessica and walked over to me. She licked my face, and I patted her on the head.

I was currently sweating through another afternoon of sixth-grade homework, my books scattered over a large blanket. I scribbled in the last few lines on my report and shoved them back into my history binder.

"Done!"

Daisy was tugging at my backpack, begging for a walk. I smiled at her. I've always wanted a dog, but it was one of the many things I had to give up as a famous world traveler.

Okay, not quite famous, but the world traveler part was spot on. You see, I'm a bit of a nomad. The only daughter of world-renowned archeologist and engineer, Russell James. Global traveler, student of the world.

Sounds great, doesn't it?

I'll admit it, some parts *are* great. Exploring remote sections of the world, making new friends, learning new languages.

But then there are the *other* parts of world travel: staying in hotels with no air conditioning and traveling to remote areas with big—I mean BIG—spiders isn't always fun. There was one time in Peru when we spotted a Giant Huntsman spider the size of a dinner plate. I had nightmares about it for weeks.

And Dad? Let's just say he's overprotective. I'm never allowed to explore anywhere on my own. I can barely get alone time in my room without him checking on me every fifteen minutes. I love him dearly, but I'd just like a little more freedom.

Daisy placed her tiny furry chin on my outstretched leg, breaking me from my thoughts.

"You ready for a walk, girl?" I scratched her head. "I'm ready for a break, too."

Daisy stood up, twirled around in a circle, and nudged at her leash.

"Jessica? Would you mind if I take Daisy for a walk?"

Jessica barely looked up. "Hmm?" Her eyes lingered on the pages of her book.

"I could use a break."

She raised her eyes to me and Daisy, who was now shaking with anticipation. "Okay. Just remember, stay close—"

"I know, I know. Don't talk to strangers and don't go into the jungle."

Jessica gave me a thin smile. "And be careful."

"Of course." I gave her my most confident grin. "Let's go, Daisy!"

I swung my favorite purple backpack over my shoulders. This wasn't just any backpack, mind you. It was decorated with patches from all over the world. Mom had given it to me, along with my first traveler's patch from France. I kept all the necessities inside; cell phone, colored pencils, a leather notebook, gum, and a headlamp—just in case.

Daisy fell in step with me as we started out across the edge of the jungle. Tikal, Guatemala, was a huge archeological site full of Mayan temples, statues, and monuments. Some of the temples extended above the tops of the trees, like lighthouses in the forest. The Mayans built one of the largest ancient cities in the world... made with no bulldozers, no cranes, and no construction equipment of any kind.

I stared out over the city. *How did they do it?*

Everything was going great—I was being completely safe—until Daisy suddenly tugged me away from the path around the Temple of the Jaguar toward a dense spot in the jungle.

"No, Daisy," I said, pulling back on her leash. "We have to stay on the path."

If I left this path, I'd never be allowed out of Dad's or Jessica's sight again.

But Daisy wasn't giving up. She pulled me into the brush and out of the sunlight. Not good. Snakes and spiders loved hanging out in the shade. I looked around nervously.

"What is it, girl?"

As my eyes adjusted to the shade, I saw a figure standing in the trees about fifteen feet away.

"Hello?" I said, my voice cracking. Daisy continued to pull me forward like a sled dog. "Daisy, will you stop?"

But she was not giving up, and I couldn't hold on any longer. The leash slipped from my hand, and she bolted into the jungle.

"Daisy!" I cried, dashing after her.

Branches and leaves whipped past me as I followed her deeper into the forest. I wasn't about to lose Daisy in the jungle, rules, or no rules.

Just as I was about to run out of breath, Daisy stopped ahead of me with an excited, *yip!*

Apparently, she had found something.

I caught up to her in a few long strides and peered into the jungle. Nestled behind a bramble of jungle leaves was a wall made of stone. After I grabbed Daisy's leash, I took a step closer.

"What did you find, girl?"

Six nooks were carved into the side of the wall, about the size of my outstretched hand. Five of the nooks had carved stones placed inside. I recognized the carvings. They were Mayan.

In fact, I had just been studying them for my history lesson.

Now I was intrigued. Maybe that report would come in handy. Dad was always going on and on about using our great knowledge of history in the field.

The first five symbols stood for Jaguar, Sun, Snake, Rain, and Skull. But the sixth nook was empty. I touched the soft grooves of the granite. My code-finding mind went to work. There must be a stone that fits into the final slot. It must follow a *logical* pattern.

What do the glyphs for Jaguar, Sun, Snake, Rain, and Skull have in common? I bit the edge of my lip. I tried to think of something useful from my report. I had taken a particular interest in the Mayan glyphs, given my love of codes and symbols.

I knew that Kinich Ahau, the god of the sun, was often depicted as a jaguar. And Chaac, the god of rain, was drawn with the body of a snake. And the skull? Well, the god of earth, and the underworld, was Cizin. He was often shown as a skull.

I felt a little chill run up my spine. Creepy.

But back to the glyphs.

Jaguar, Sun, Snake, Rain, Skull... Earth?

It was worth a shot.

There were stones scattered about the jungle floor and I quickly shifted through them, looking for earth symbol. A few were broken, some had parts of a carving. They represented everything from rain drops to mountains.

Then I stumbled over a sharp object jutting out of the jungle floor. I got down on my knees. I could see a stone half-buried in the mud. I dug my fingers into the ground and began to dig. When I was done, I stared at the stone.

It had the symbol for earth. Bingo!

I ran back to the center of the wall and placed it in the sixth nook. To my surprise, it fit perfectly in place.

Then something weird happened. The ground beneath began to rumble.

Was this an earthquake?

It wasn't that unusual for an earthquake to happen in Central America. But right after I placed the sixth symbol? That was a little odd.

The stones in front of me suddenly began to move, and I pulled Daisy back as several rocks began to fall. We huddled together near the ground. I placed my hands over my head and squeezed my eyes shut. A few seconds later, the shaking stopped.

I looked up. The center of the wall that held the carved stones had crumbled into a pile at my feet.

So much for solving that riddle.

"Come on, Daisy, we better get back," I said, pulling on her leash.

If my overprotective dad knew I was by myself in the jungle during an earthquake?

I shuddered at the thought.

But just as I was about to leave, my eyes caught on a peculiar green glow coming from the pile of stones.

Daisy must have noticed it too, because she walked back over to the spot. As she sniffed the ground, I saw she was standing over a small object that appeared to be lit from within. I squatted down and took a closer look.

It was a little statue, about as big as an eggplant. I reached down and touched it, feeling the cool surface on my skin. Perhaps it was made of jade?

I could hear Dad's voice in my head shouting, *You should be wearing gloves!*

Well, he wasn't here, so I picked it up.

It had to be a real Mayan artifact. What else would it be doing here in the jungle?

Then I got that weird feeling you get when someone's watching you. I spun around and looked every which way I could. Leaves were moving off toward the temple as if someone had just parted them.

I figured I had a few choices. I could run the piece back to Dad and share my discovery. That would be the obvious thing to do.

Or I could do some research of my own, find out who this little guy was. Maybe if I found out enough, I could convince Dad that I was old enough to explore on my own.

What should I do?

One thing I did know was I had to get out of there. The waving tree limbs gave me the heebie-jeebies.

And then, the answer hit me.

I'd pay a visit to my friend, Aly, whose parents managed one of the museums here in Tikal. She could help me figure out what it was.

"What do you think, Daisy girl? Should we get out of here? Check this one out ourselves?"

Daisy yipped back, obviously agreeing with me.

I stashed the statue in my backpack and set off towards our rental house in the village. First, I had to stop at home and enter this week's answer for the cryptography competition. After that, we'd head over to the museum.

I didn't know it at the time, but that little statue I had stuffed in my backpack?

It was about to get me into a whole world of trouble.

CHAPTER 2

THE BOY WITH THE BRITISH ACCENT

My pace slowed as I neared the entrance of the museum. The building itself had a low, flat roof and was decorated with wood slats on the outside walls with turquoise panels in between. I'd spent lots of time walking through the various exhibits inside with Aly. She showed me all the cool historical finds of Mayan history, even the ones that weren't on display.

And the air conditioning was a bonus.

But what caused me to pause today were the two police officers I saw standing outside the building, talking with Aly's parents, Mr. and Mrs. Reyes.

Mrs. Reyes saw me approaching. "¡Hola, Harley! ¿Como estas?" She gave me a big smile.

"Hola, Mrs. Reyes. I'm fine, and you?"

"Bien," she replied. Then, knowing my limited Spanish, she switched to English. "If you're looking for Aly, she's around back, playing fetch with Nacho."

"Right, thank you," I said.

Mrs. Reyes nodded and returned her attention to the police.

As I rounded the corner, I saw Aly on the large grassy area behind the museum. She was wearing her T-shirt with the puppy on the front.

Aly and I met a few months ago when Dad and I arrived for an excavation. We bonded over our love of dogs and lifestyle. Aly loved hearing the stories of my travels around the world, from Turkey to Egypt to Japan, and I lived vicariously through her by hearing the latest gossip from her school. She was currently on spring break, so it was doubtful she'd have any new gossip to catch me up on.

Daisy ran up to Aly and Nacho.

"Hey, Aly," I said.

"Harley! Come on back!" She gestured me toward the field where she and Nacho were playing. Unlike little Daisy, who pushed the scales at ten pounds, Nacho weighed about forty-five pounds. He bounded forward to greet us. Aly had Nacho's favorite toy, a neon green Frisbee.

"So, what's with the police?" I asked.

"Oh, that." She wiped the beads of sweat from her brow. Spring in Guatemala was quite warm. It was nearly eighty degrees and full-on humidity in the jungle. "There's been some trouble at the museum."

A weird chill ran through me. "What kind of trouble?"

"Some of the jade jewelry from the burial collection is missing."

"Missing, as in stolen?" Aly told me the last time they had anyone steal anything was when someone took the Goddess of Luck and then went on a spending spree, buying lottery tickets. As it turned out, another tourist spotted the man buying tickets in the gas station and recognized the statue. The burglar went to jail, and the Goddess of Luck was returned home.

Not so lucky, after all.

"Yeah. It's terrible!" She tossed the Frisbee into the air, which whipped around sideways and landed flat on the ground. Apparently, Aly wasn't so coordinated.

"My parents had security cameras installed, but they did not show anything. I guess the pieces are worth a lot of money."

"That stinks." There was a pretty strong black market in Guatemala for artifacts, from what Dad said.

I continued to watch as Daisy and Nacho happily chased each other in the grass.

"Tell me about it," Aly said. "They reported it to the police, but they are not very hopeful that the police can help. The police said they were professionals." Aly tugged at the end of her long, black braid, untangling it from her shirt.

"Well, maybe I can help. I'm pretty good at solving puzzles," I said, trying to cheer her up.

"Thanks for the offer, but..."

Aly stopped mid-sentence as she saw a boy walking toward us from the direction of the museum. He was taller than me by at least six inches and maybe a few years older. He had hair the color of Cheetos and his skin looked like an alabaster statue.

"Hello," he said, giving us an awkward wave. "I'm looking for Alejandra?"

"That's me," Aly said, waving back.

"My name is Deacon. Your mother sent me to fetch you. She said you might show me 'round the museum?"

He definitely had a British accent. And what kid said, "fetch?"

Was he another kid along for the dig?

"Oh yeah, sure, just give me a sec." Aly looked back at me and raised her eyebrows.

There aren't a lot of kids around ancient cities, except for the tourists. With his khaki color shirt and worn boots, he didn't look much like a tourist. He was also wearing an interesting-looking gold medallion around his neck, tied with a leather cord.

I decided to introduce myself.

"Hi, I'm Harley." I stepped in his direction, extending my hand. "I'm staying over in the Tulum Village with my dad, who is..."

To my surprise, Deacon cut me off and narrowed his eyes. "I know who you are."

He was just a few feet from me and ignored my extended hand; instead, he just stared at me. I let my hand drop to my side, then opened my mouth to respond, but reconsidered.

What did I ever do to this guy?

Aly looked at him, then back at me. I was just about to ask him why he was being so rude when I heard a familiar voice.

"Harley! There you are!"

I turned around to see Dad hurrying toward us, huffing and puffing. He was still wearing his field clothes and a khaki fedora firmly planted on his head. He pulled out his handkerchief and wiped the sweat from his forehead.

"Hi Dad, I was just..."

He waved me into silence and then paused a moment, catching his breath. "I was worried when you didn't come back. Jessica said, you went for a walk. Can you please check in with me next time?"

"Yes, I'm sorry. I just—"

"It's okay. Just please let me know next time." He pulled out his water bottle and took a long drink. "Listen, it's almost dinner time. Let's go home, okay?"

I understand why Dad is the way he is. I'm all he has. When I was little Mom and Dad used to pack me up and tote me around the world. But when Mom got cancer, everything changed. We made a home in Ohio and things seemed to get better. But then they didn't. And one day, my mom died. It was really hard on both of us.

Dad fumbled around for six months, hardly leaving the house. I was sad too, but I was even more worried about him. Then one day he scooped me up, and we began our grand adventure. We figured out school and all the other bits as we went along.

I adjusted the weight of my backpack, feeling the contents shift inside. I hadn't gotten to show Aly the statue. Still, now wasn't the time. I kept my mouth shut. I wasn't about to share it with her now that Deacon was here. He was still casting glaring looks at me.

What is with him? He had leaned down at Nacho's feet and was scratching between his ears. Nice to Aly. Nice to Nacho and Daisy.

Why so rude to me?

"Okay." I made eye contact with Aly. "I'll come by tomorrow."

Aly nodded in response, a smile on her face. "Adios, mi amiga."

"Adios," I replied, giving one last look to Deacon as I walked away. He kept his back to me, focused on Nacho. I turned and followed Dad and Daisy back to the village.

I had to jog a bit to keep up with them.

"Who was the new kid?" he asked over his shoulder. "A tourist?"

"I don't know." I shrugged. "But he had a British accent."

"Oh, he's probably with the new group that just arrived on Friday from the Royal Archeological Institute."

Well, that makes sense.

Normally, I would have been thrilled to have another kid around my age on a dig site. Deacon, however, showed little promise as a friend. I kept my opinion of him to myself, and we walked the rest of the way in silence.

As we approached the place we were currently calling home, Daisy yipped to attention and pulled on her leash. She was looking toward the jungle brush and ignoring Jessica, who was heading to meet us. I followed her gaze. Once again, I noticed leaves swaying on a branch.

And there was no breeze.

"Come on, Daisy," Jessica said as she took her leash and pulled her towards the village. I looked back at the jungle and had the same weird feeling I had earlier.

This time I was sure of it.

We were being followed.

CHAPTER 3

TO STASH A STATUE

Ipoked at my dinner, a concoction of rice, tortillas, and shredded beef in tomato sauce. It was a traditional Guatemalan meal called Hilachas, which I normally devoured. But tonight, I was lost in thought. So many things had happened today.

The statue I'd found and stashed in my room.

The missing jade artifacts from the museum.

This new kid, Deacon. What a jerk.

It was all I could think about. I wondered whether all the events were connected somehow.

Daisy lay on the floor next to my feet, waiting for a spare crumb. Dad and I sat next to each other at one end of the table and Jessica at the other side. She often joined us for dinner when she wasn't video chatting with her boyfriend from the States.

"Peso for your thoughts, Harley?" Dad was staring at me. He was wearing his signature blue button-down field shirt with a red bandana tied around his neck. His mousy brown hair was past due

20

for a cut, but I still thought my dad was the most handsome archeologist there is. Besides *Indiana Jones,* of course.

"Just thinking about something Aly told me. Some jade pieces that got stolen from the museum."

I left out the part about the statue I'd found. I was still trying to sort out how I was going to leverage my lucky find to impress Dad. He was going to be blown away when I told him about the four Mayan symbols I found in the jungle, not to mention the statue itself.

"Don't worry, sweetie. It will all get sorted out," Dad said, giving a sideways glance at Jessica. I knew that look well. It was the look he gave when there was some type of adult issue he thought was over my head. I was sick of him always doing that. If he was going to drag me along on these adventures, then I had a right to know things.

"Why would someone steal them?"

Dad had his mouth full, so Jessica jumped in to answer. She was from Guatemala originally, just two hours north of Tikal. As a graduate student of archeology, she knew loads of stuff about the Maya.

"Authentic jade jewelry, especially from the early Mayan period, is worth a lot of money. Sometimes many thousands of dollars. Unfortunately, looters like to steal artifacts and sell them."

"On the black market?"

"Exactly," Dad said, finally swallowing his mouthful. "In this case, most likely to private collectors or organizations." He leaned back in his painted chair and wiped his mouth. "It's very frustrating, but it happens."

As I listened to them speak, a million more questions rattled around in my head. It was all the more reason to keep the statue a secret.

"Do you think the thieves are dangerous?"

Dad's face tightened. That look said everything I needed to know.

"Yes," said my father. "But it's nothing you have to worry about, Harley."

Before I could ask more questions, Dad changed the subject. "I just heard a new joke today. Would you like to hear it?"

I tried not to roll my eyes. Dad and his friends at the dig site loved to come up with jokes as they stood around sifting dirt. They were usually bad, but often so silly, I had to laugh despite myself.

"Sure."

"What do you call a Mayan snake tied in a knot?"

"I have no idea," I said, trying to give him an attentive look.

"Pretzel-coatal." His eyes lit up as he delivered the punch line.

I laughed, more at how pleased Dad was with himself than at the actual joke.

"You know the actual name is Kukulcán, Dad," I said, giving him a good-natured jab in the arm.

"Now that is impressive, Harley. You're correct." Dad's smile grew. "Sounds like your Mayan studies are coming along nicely."

I nodded as I plunged my fork into a chunk of beef. "We learned about Mayan hieroglyphics today."

"Oh, really?" Dad asked. "Can you tell me how many glyphs the Mayans had in their alphabet?"

Dad *loved* to quiz me on history. Whenever we visited a site, he always gave me a book about the area, its history, and culture.

"Around 800," I replied.

"That's right," he said, his face breaking into a wide smile. "And can you tell me what they call a Mayan book?"

"A codex." I smiled back.

"Correct! You are one smart girl, Cat-Cat."

Cat-Cat was his pet name for me. Ironic, given I love dogs. Daisy stirred at my feet. The word "cat" put her on guard.

"We're very close to making an important discovery here." Dad put down his fork as he spoke. I looked at the dark circles under his eyes. He'd been working really hard, spending long hours at the site. Despite that, he had a glint in his eye.

I cocked my head in curiosity. "What kind of discovery?"

"Using our drones, we've found a new site just north of Tikal. A burial site, one that would've been missed otherwise."

Dad rattled on about how psyched they were. He had helped develop a laser technology that took pictures from the sky. It was like an x-ray of the surface of the earth, taken by a drone. And it allowed archeologists and scientists to see through the thick plants of the jungle to the ancient ruins underneath. Burial sites often brought the most information about a culture from the past.

"And get this, Cat-Cat. We found two small jade statues, which we believe represent two of the Three Kings of this region."

"Statues?" I squeaked, dropping my fork and nearly choking on a mouthful of rice and beans. I pounded my chest to make the food go down.

"Yes," continued my father. "It was very exciting. We chopped through brush as tall as our heads. We came across no less than four highly venomous snakes. At one point, I stepped into a termite hole and was pretty sure I was done for."

I cocked my head and smiled at Dad. He had a flair for telling dramatic stories, in addition to his corny jokes. But I couldn't help but notice his mention of statues.

"What about the statues?" I asked.

"We believe there's a third statue, but we haven't been able to locate it." He paused. "But if we had all three, it would be a huge win for our research. We have until Friday to find the third statue before we meet the grant review board."

My cheeks flushed red. My head swirled with thoughts.

Should I tell them? Should I stick to my plan?

I swallowed, sitting up straight and trying to compose myself. "That's great, Dad."

Jessica gave me a concerned look. "Harley, are you alright?"

"Of course," I said, gulping down some water. I had to give the statue to Dad. "May I be excused? I'm feeling a little tired tonight."

"Sure, honey," said Dad. "I'll be in to say goodnight later."

I headed back to my bedroom—which I was really happy to have. Most of the time, we couldn't afford places with bedrooms. But this time we were staying in an actual house. True, there was no air conditioning, but the fan helped relieve the jungle heat.

The room had a twin bed, a nightstand with a small lamp, and a turquoise dresser. Daisy followed me in. I was on my knees in seconds, my hands searching underneath the bed. When I came home for dinner, I'd wrapped the statue in my favorite purple T-shirt and stashed it there. I reached in for it...... and my hands came out empty. I grabbed my cell phone off the nightstand, dropped it to my belly, and shined the light under the bed.

Daisy sensed my anxiety and put her nose to work as well, sniffing around the bed and nightstand. I was *sure* I had left it under my bed. It was just here, what, an hour ago?

I looked again, crawling in deeper. There was nothing but dust bunnies. The statue I'd found today—the one that was to be a huge 'win' for Dad's research?

It was gone.

CHAPTER 4

THE MISSING STATUE

The next morning, I stared at the ceiling of my bedroom. I'd been up all night, worried about looters sneaking in my room. And here I'd had the very thing Dad needed for his trip to be successful. Why had I hidden it away instead of showing him? For some stupid reason, like him giving me more freedom to roam alone. What had I been thinking? My bad choices had ruined everything.

Where had that little statue gone?

There were two options. One, someone inside the house had found the statue and taken it. Despite the house being tiny, it still had three bedrooms, a kitchen, a living room, and a small bathroom. Dad, Jessica, and I were all in the kitchen together, having dinner, when the statue went missing. There was only one door in and out. And we were sitting right next to it.

So option one was out.

The second option was that someone followed me home, snuck into my room, and retrieved the statue from under my bed. This sent a chill up my spine. I had a window in my bedroom, just above my bed. It wouldn't have been easy, but someone could have opened the window, crawled inside, and pulled the statue from under my bed. And I did have that feeling I was being followed.

But how had they done it without me noticing? Even if I hadn't noticed, Daisy would have. She'd have barked and gone crazy.

I looked at the window next to me and decided to try out the theory for myself. The window itself was cracked, enough to let some cool air breeze through the room while I slept. But the screen on the outside was shut tightly.

I positioned myself on my knees, reached up, and opened up the window all the way to the top. Next, I propped my hands underneath the top screen and pushed.

I gave it all the strength I had.

The screen didn't budge. I checked the latch. It was definitely unlocked. I heaved on it one more time, and still nothing. It seemed as if the screen had been painted shut. It didn't look like it had been opened in a decade. There was no way someone would have made it through the window without us hearing.

I sat back on my heels, wondering what to do next.

"Harley!" Jessica's voice interrupted my thoughts. "Your breakfast is ready."

I decided there wasn't much else to do, so I grabbed my backpack and headed towards the kitchen. Maybe some food would help my brain come up with more ideas.

Jessica wasn't in the kitchen, but I spotted some food on the table. I piled some scrambled eggs on my fork and shoved them in my mouth. Just like I couldn't sleep, I didn't feel like eating. But I did have a pretty big day ahead of me. Jessica was taking me out to the dig site to meet Dad.

A few moments later, Jessica emerged from her bedroom, Daisy in tow.

"Ready to go, Daisy girl?" I said.

The dog yipped in excitement.

Dad had already left for the day, heading to a dig site where they'd meet with local archeologists to help with their map findings. That left me and Jessica, and she was furiously texting with her boyfriend. She'd told me he was a senior at UCLA, working on his degree in biology. They were pretty obsessed with each other. I assumed it was him.

"Jessica, is it okay if I take Daisy on a quick walk?"

She looked up at me and nodded. "Sure, Harley, that's fine. Please—"

"Be careful, I know."

She gave me a knowing look before turning back to her phone.

Daisy and I stepped out the door. The temperature was already rising in the jungle. I could feel the humidity wrap around me like a blanket. Our little rental house was nestled in a clearing, the edges of which gave way to dense bushes, trees, and grasses. One of the first things I had noticed about living here was that the jungle was *loud*.

I could hear everything. Howler monkeys bellowed their songs at night, sometimes keeping me awake. The mornings were full of the sounds of the birds singing and chirping. And don't even get me started on the frogs and insects. Daisy bounded forward, full of energy. She loved to chase the lizards through the clearing where all the little rental houses huddled together.

We rounded the corner of the house, walking around the back near my bedroom window. Daisy had her nose to the ground, searching for the next lizard. She suddenly jerked the leash.

"Daisy?" I pulled her back. "What is it?"

Following the trajectory of her nose, I caught sight of something out of place, just below my window. I bent down to see what it was.

Footprints.

There were small boot prints in the ground. I looked closer. The pattern on the print had a star shape in the center. My heart jumped up in my throat. Maybe someone *had* tried to break into my bedroom window.

I placed my shoe gingerly inside one of the boot prints. It's a near-perfect match. Which made me wonder, *Was this the boot print of a child? Surely an adult wouldn't have feet this small.*

I gazed around the clearing at the other houses. There were about a dozen houses in the clearing, all painted different pastel colors. All the homes were rentals, so people like Dad and I could be comfortable for longer stays. I wasn't sure who else was staying in this area, but maybe someone had seen something that would help. Not like I was going to go door to door to ask.

Daisy and I followed the boot prints to the edge of the woods. They disappeared there. And I wasn't about to dive into the jungle.

Did you know there are eighteen species of poisonous snakes in Guatemala? Just the idea of snakes and insects made me shiver.

"Harley, right?"

I jumped, dropping Daisy's leash in the process. I jerked my head around to see where the voice had come from.

It was the rude boy from yesterday, Deacon. Out in the full sun, his hair glowed like a matchstick on top of his head.

"Yes." I tried to sound calm like he hadn't just scared me out of my boots. "Harley James."

"What are you doing out here, Harley James?"

"Well, I was just—" But then Daisy lunged towards the jungle, dragging her leash behind her. I ran after her, calling her name. Daisy had snake training, but Jessica would kill me if I lost her in the woods.

Just as I was about to reach her, I slid into a puddle of mud and went down face-first. I managed to catch myself with my elbows, but the splash of muck splattered all over my face and clothes.

Deacon raced past me, calling for Daisy as she sped away. He was able to grab her leash just before she disappeared in the brush. He walked her back to where I sat.

I watched him come towards me as I wiped the mud from my hands and face. He was wearing cargo shorts, a red polo, and hiking boots. I wondered if he was heading to the dig site today as well. He was a bit out of breath as he handed me the leash.

"Thanks."

"You're welcome."

I saw a slight lift of his lips as he said it. My cheeks burned red. He turned away from me then, heading back towards a blue house that was nestled on the edge of the clearing. "See you around."

I pulled Daisy back to my side and watched as Deacon walked away. I noticed he was wearing a gold medallion hanging from a leather string. Maybe it was some kind of good luck charm?

That's one strange boy. But at least he hadn't been rude today.

Daisy and I stepped up our pace as we walked back to the house. Jessica would be waiting on me, and I was going to need to change my clothes before we left.

It was clear to me now that someone had stolen the statue from my room, and the boot prints were my only clue as to who it might be. I looked again towards the blue house Deacon had disappeared into.

Whoever had taken it, I was determined to get it back. I would stop at nothing until I had it in my purple backpack.

The bad news? I only had until Friday morning.

CHAPTER 5

THREE KINGS OF THE MAYA

"Hold on, Harley!" Jessica shouted as we bumped along the road into the jungle. Actually, the road was the wrong word. It was more like a dirt path barely wide enough for two people to walk next to each other, let alone ride in a Jeep, like the one we were in.

The palm fronds and branches slapped against the sides. Our little Jeep was just one in a caravan of vehicles. I held my backpack tightly to my chest while another pothole bounced us up into the air and we dropped back down to earth.

This is a perfect example of how un-glamourous exploration can be. Not only was it a rocky ride to the dig site, but the sun was beating down on us through the open top of the jeep. I was already sweating through my blue T-shirt.

"Would you mind telling me about the legend of the Three Mayan Kings?" I asked Jessica.

She glanced at me while keeping her hands firmly on the wheel. "Would you like the textbook version or the local legend with the haunted ghosts?"

My pulse quickened. "Both."

"Well, there were three regions of this area, ruled by Mayan Kings. Jasaw, Yax K'uk, and Jacinto. Each of these kings ruled ruthlessly. When they conquered each other's lands, they took prisoners. Let's just say prisoners weren't treated so well, and often they were killed."

"That's awful."

Jessica shrugged. "Awful, but true. At the time, the Mayan people believed the gods had anointed their kings, so they were willing to go along with just about anything."

Another bump on the road jolted us into the air. I gripped the handrail above me to steady myself. Jessica continued, unfazed.

"Now, here's where the textbook version ends, and the legend begins. It's said that the Mayan people grew angry as the kings battled for supremacy. They overthrew the guards and killed the Three Kings. In order to keep the kings from ever returning, they carved three jade statues and placed the kings' hearts inside them."

"For real?" That was gross. But the statue had been about the right size to hold a heart.

A human heart.

"Pretty nasty, right? According to the legend, they divided up the three statues and hid them in different places because, if they were ever altogether, the spirits of the Three Kings might return and raise armies to rule the land once again."

As she said it, a breeze blew through the open air of the Jeep, and goosebumps broke out on my skin.

"Do you think it's true?"

She shrugged. "Who knows? There are all sorts of legends passed down through the Maya. Some we can confirm through discoveries like your dad has made. With others? We may never know." Jessica took one hand off the wheel and wiped some sweat from her temples. "Regardless, people have been searching for the Three

Kings of the Maya for hundreds of years. It would be a massive achievement if we were to find all three."

We sat in silence for the rest of the ride. Sweat ran down my back even though a slight breeze flowed over the windshield. I'd been looking forward to meeting Dad, but now? Not so much. I had single-handedly lost one of the most significant discoveries in Mayan history, all because I wanted to prove to Dad that I was independent enough to be out on my own.

Way to go, Harley.

The Jeep slowed to a crawl as we approached the site.

That's when I noticed a loud chirping, beating in a perfect rhythm. We jumped out of the car.

"What in the world is that noise?" I practically had to yell for Jessica to hear me.

"Cicadas," Jessica replied, leaning in so I could hear her. "They crawl out from the ground every spring to mate."

"Why are they so loud?"

"I'm not sure. Usually, they don't emerge for another three months, but they came out early this year. Just yesterday, actually. Right after they discovered the statues."

That's awfully strange timing, I thought as I walked behind her.

A group of archeologists, excavators, and local people had been working for days to dig out the new structures. Today was what Dad liked to call "on-the-job training." It was part of my schooling, and he insisted on it once a week. At first, I thought I'd be able to just walk around and look at stuff, but he put a stop to that on the first day. At a bare minimum, I usually ended up carrying dirt from one place to another or sorting and organizing materials.

There were about two dozen people working at the site, all bent over large rectangular holes in the ground. Archaeologists study past human activity by excavating, dating, and interpreting objects and sites of historical interest. My "on-the-job training" had taught me that it was a lot of slow, tedious work, and it took a whole team of people to do it.

"Harley!" I heard a familiar voice as we came to a halt.

Aly was waving. Next to her was her brother, Ricardo, who was a few years older than she was. He flashed pearly white teeth at all the girls who came by the museum, charming them with his smile. The girls hung around, laughing loudly at his jokes, and acting ridiculous.

I found this all very silly.

Okay, fine, I thought he was a little bit cute, too, but I would never admit this to Aly.

"Aly! Ricardo!" I jumped out of the Jeep and bounded towards them. "What are you doing here?"

"Mama and Papa said we could come help today," said Aly brightly. "I'm so glad you're here!"

I could hear Jessica's footsteps crunching in the jungle brush behind me.

"Jessica, you remember Aly and Ricardo?"

"Hola," said Jessica, then she turned her attention to the group of archeologists at the farthest hole. I followed her gaze and saw a collection of makeshift tents scattered over a large rectangular grid, with strings pulled tightly. There were wheelbarrows, tables, and buckets of dirt all lined up neatly on the side. The entire clearing was about the size of a baseball diamond.

"Harley, let's join your dad and see what they have for you to do today."

Images of hauling dirt filled my mind.

"Can I stay with Aly and Ricardo? Work on the dig with them?" I gave her my best hopeful puppy face, the same one that Daisy gives to me when she wants table scraps. "Please? I'm sure I'll learn a ton."

"We're working right over there," Aly said, pointing towards the northeast corner of the site.

"Please?"

"Alright," Jessica said finally. "Just make sure you're back over with our group by lunch. I'll want a full report of what you worked on."

"A written report?" I asked, feeling dread clench my stomach.

Even Jessica laughed at the horror on my face. "No. Just, let's say, five minutes with facts. Now go on. And here, take Daisy with you."

I took the leash, and Daisy jumped up and pressed her paws against my knees in excitement.

"Yes, ma'am." I saluted her. "Five minutes. With facts."

Jessica gave me a thin smile and headed to the northwest, to the larger group.

"Come on, Harley," said Aly. "I'll show you what we are working on."

Ricardo and Aly led me to the smaller excavation site. They both wore cargo pants and hiking boots like mine, with trowels and brushes weighing down their pockets.

Ricardo started talking about the history of their particular site as we fell into a straight line along the path. It was here they had discovered the two statues buried under a pile of rubble, and they believed were moved here by looters hundreds of years ago.

As we walked, we left prints in the soft dirt. Ricardo's. Then Aly's. Then mine. Aly's boot prints were almost the same size as mine. I looked closer. They had a star shape in the center, just like the prints...

I stopped in my tracks.

Had Aly broken into my room last night?

CHAPTER 6
LET'S PLAY BALL

"Harley, you okay?"

Aly noticed my hesitation and turned back. Thinking quickly, I bent down and untied my boot.

"Um, I think I have a stone." I made a quick show of pulling off the boot, turning it upside down, and pounding it. Then I put it back on, retied it, and brushed off my shorts. "Much better."

Aly smiled and turned to follow the rest of the group. We walked through the jungle for about ten minutes, following a muddy path that squished beneath my boots. The adults at the front of the group carried machetes that they used to hack away at anything in our way.

Large palm leaves swept over our heads like a big green umbrella shielding us from the sun. Daisy pulled at the end of her leash, sniffing the ground for bugs, snakes, and anything else that might be skittering across the path.

"We're here!" Aly said triumphantly as we slowed to a stop. A set of massive stone steps covered in bright green moss rose up ahead of us.

"Careful, Harley, it's slippery!" Ricardo called back as I stumbled up the steps.

As we reached the top, I looked down the large rectangular pit that opened up before us. It was about half the size of a soccer field. On each side, stone walls angled up toward the sky. The stones were stacked together like a giant game of Tetris, with jungle vines weaving through them.

"Do you recognize it?" asked Aly.

"Recognize what?" I said, staring down below.

"This," she pointed to the large pit and sloped stone walls. "It's a Mayan ball court where they played Poc-a-Toc. There's at least one in every Mayan city."

"Cool!" My curiosity pushed away thoughts of the boot print. This was definitely something I could report back to Jessica at lunch. "How did they play?"

"There isn't a direct account of how the games were played. But, from what historians can put together, two teams played with a rubber ball, trying to send the ball through the loop at the top of the slope there." She pointed to a large stone circle, about three feet across, at the top of the slope.

"Did they throw the ball?"

"No, they couldn't use their hands or feet. So they had to use their hips, shoulders, knees, or elbows."

"Kind of like soccer?"

"Yes. But with one big difference."

"What's that?" I asked.

"It was to the death," she said, widening her eyes for effect. "The winners killed the losers."

"No!" My hand flew up to cover my mouth.

"Yes. They sacrificed the losers to the gods."

"That's terrible!"

"Yeah, Ricardo gets pretty serious about soccer, but this was on a whole other level." Aly said as she pulled her backpack around her shoulder. She stuck her hand inside. "Banana?"

My stomach did a loopty-loo. "No, I'm good."

"Aly, stop trying to scare her," Ricardo called from across the pit. "Come over here, you two. I want to show you something."

I took a few photos with my phone as we walked. There were engravings of players in elaborate headgear kneeling before their gods, the ball flying through the air, spectators watching from afar. This would be great material to show Jessica when we broke for lunch.

Aly and I made our way across the edge of the pit between the drop-off and the sloped wall. As we grew closer, I could see one of the adults from the dig crew was holding something in his hands.

I recognized it instantly. The color of the bone, the empty sockets where eyes used to be, the discolored set of teeth.

"A skull," I whispered out as we neared the group. I had been to my fair share of archeology sites, but the sight of a skull still gave me the willies.

"Not just one skull, there is a whole pit full of skulls and bones," said Ricardo, brushing a thick strand of hair from his eyes. We peered over the side of a smaller pit, where half a dozen workers were sifting through the dirt for bones. "Apparently, this is where you ended up if you lost the game."

"I thought games were supposed to be fun?" I said, adjusting my backpack on my shoulders as I looked inside.

"I'm sure it was fun," said Aly, raising her brows. "If you were on the winning team."

"Right," I said, a slight shiver going up my spine. Sports have never been my strong suit. Good thing I wasn't born during the time of the ancient Maya.

Ricardo was speaking in his native tongue with a group of archeologists. I caught bits and pieces of what they were saying, but my Spanish was pretty basic.

"They need some help laying out tarps over there," he said, gesturing towards the other end of the dig. "So they can count the bones."

Aly and Ricardo set off towards a pile of neatly stacked, bright blue tarps. I started to follow but then noticed the boot prints that Aly had left behind. There was no doubt about it. Not only were they the same size as mine, but they also had the star in the center.

I decided my best approach would be to address the situation head-on.

"So my dad was telling me about some statues they'd found. The Three Kings of Tikal?"

Aly was unfolding a large blue plastic tarp out over the ground. I grabbed the side of it to help her. "Yeah. My parents have been talking about them as well. They found two of the legendary Mayan kings."

"What about the third?" My voice caught in my throat. I could feel the sweat tickle my palms.

Aly shook her head. "Never been found."

She tugged at the edge of the tarp, trying to use a metal stake to secure it to the ground. I watched her face closely.

It didn't seem like she was lying. She was looking right at me and not shifting or glancing away when she talked like liars do.

Daisy was panting by my side.

"Missing like the pieces from the museum?"

"The pieces from the museum have been in our collection for a long time. The Three Kings of Tikal have never been found. Apparently, the first two statues had been looted from a gravesite a few hundred years ago and then vanished. That is what we found over where your dad has been digging." She paused and pulled out a bottle of water. "But the third statue was said to be hidden in a secret location in the jungle." Her eyes twinkled, and she lowered her voice. "Hidden with a magic spell."

"Magic?"

"Yes, there are those who believe in the *Leyenda de los Tres Reyes...* The Legend of the Three Kings. But it's more of a curse."

"A curse?"

"The legend says when the kings are united on the eve of the thirteenth Baktun, their ghosts will return to Earth and take revenge on the ancestors of their people."

"Jessica said that they would return and rule over the land."

"Well," said Aly, shrugging her shoulders, "there are lots of different versions of the story. But they all say the same thing—the kings must not be reunited."

Ricardo hurried over to the two of us with a mallet. We hadn't had much luck pushing our stakes in the ground. "I heard that the ghosts of the Three Kings will return with an army of Mayan zombies. And bring on the Apocalypse the Mayan calendar predicted."

"And you think I am the one who is going to scare her?" Aly asked.

Ricardo laughed, and he used the mallet to secure the stake in place.

"I thought the time for the Mayan apocalypse had already passed? Wasn't that in 2012?" I asked.

"Some Mayans believe that those predictions were off... by about ten years," said Ricardo.

"But that would mean..."

"That the apocalypse would happen this year, in 2022. In fact, some people have calculated the Baktun will arrive this Friday."

The same day my father is supposed to present the three statues. I swallowed.

"Oh, don't listen to him, Harley. He's just trying to scare you."

Ricardo shrugged. "It's just a theory."

"Come on, let's find your dad and then get lunch. I am starving," Aly swiveled around and began to hike back the way we'd come. I turned to follow her, but Daisy tugged at my leash, pulling me back towards the jungle. She began barking.

"What is it, Daisy?"

I took a step toward the jungle with her and heard something crunch underneath my feet. I looked down and found a small piece of notebook paper, folded over several times. I scooped it up and unfolded it.

The resemblance was unmistakable. It was a drawing of the very same statuette I had found yesterday.

The third Mayan King.

"Harley?" called Aly, who was now about fifteen feet away.

"Right behind you!" I called. I crumpled up the piece of paper and shoved it into my backpack.

Whoever had made this sketch must have something to do with the missing statue. I didn't know if that person was Aly or maybe even Ricardo. But somehow, I'd figure out a way to find out.

CHAPTER 7
LOST LEGENDS OF
THE MAYA

L ate that night, I snuck into the living room and pulled my
laptop off the charger. Dad had gone to bed, but I could see
the light on from Jessica's room. She was probably Face
Timing with her boyfriend.

I hugged the laptop to my chest as I skittered back into my
room. Once I was inside, I quietly shut the door and crawled into
bed. After making a small tent with my blanket, I opened up the
cover and found the Google search bar. I typed in the Legend of the
Three Mayan Kings.

Over twelve million results. Ugh.

There was a *lot* of information to sort through. The ghosts of
human sacrifices, the long-lost gods, and much more. But I couldn't
find much that specifically related to the Three Kings. I changed my
approach and typed in *Leyenda de los Tres Reyes.*

I found a page with the exact same title.

Bingo.

My heart felt like it was going to push through my skin and
pound out of my chest.

There it was: The Legend of the Three Mayan Kings. I read through the passage:

Leyenda de los Tres Reyes says that the Three Kings, Jasaw, Yax K'uk, and Jacinto, were murdered in a coup by their people on the night of the first Baktun. In honor of their victory over the unjust rule of the kings, the people had three jade statues commissioned to commemorate the defeat.

Legend says their hearts were torn out and placed inside of each statuette; however, there is no official record of this act. The three statues were separated and taken to the farthest boundaries of each of the three kingdoms in order to ensure their spirits would never be reunited, for separated they were powerless, but together they could destroy the world. The statues have never been recovered.

I scrolled down to the bottom, hoping for more information, such as how the statues were hidden. But there was nothing. I went back to the search results and scanned a few more pages, but the information was just a repeat of what Jessica had told me word-for-word.

I pushed my laptop aside and reached for my backpack to retrieve the folded note I had found earlier that day. Just as I was about to pull it back under the covers, I heard a noise.

Tap, tap, tap.

It sounded like it was coming from my window. I quickly turned off the light from my flashlight and pulled the covers back over my head. I was too scared to look. What if it was the looters? Or even worse...

What if it was the ghosts of the Three Kings?

Okay, I knew that was ridiculous. And impossible. Even so, the story had been scary, and everyone else was asleep. Every part of me wanted to bolt for Dad's bedroom, but I was too terrified to move. I tried the deep breathing my counselor had taught me after mom died.

This calmed me some.

The noise stopped. I thought I could maybe inch toward Dad's room while staying under the covers. I moved ever so slightly.

Then I heard something that stopped me in my tracks.

Slap.

The sound was so different from the other one that I took a chance and lifted the blanket to peek. What I saw was a small hand with a note pushed up against the window. The note read:

Come outside! -Aly

I sat back and took a deep breath, slapping my hand to my head and feeling like a complete idiot. It wasn't the looters, and it sure wasn't the ghosts of three dead kings. It was Aly. I shrugged off the rest of the blanket and used the flashlight to find my shoes. I snagged my backpack also, just in case. I was still wearing my pajama shorts and the university T-shirt that I slept in, but it would have to do.

"Harley, over here." Aly kept her voice in a low whisper.

I rounded the corner to the back of the house and flicked off my flashlight. The village lampposts cast a low light around the space. Aly stood next to my window. There was a collection of new boot prints with the star under my window... and she was wearing boots!

"Aly, what are you doing here?"

The light from a lamppost caught a glint in her eye as she spoke. "I came to find you. I saw the light glowing from your window. There is something I need to show you."

"Okay, but it's pretty late," I scanned the dark clearing as I spoke. "And—"

I paused. Could I trust Aly? I hated to even ask the question...

"And what?" Aly's head cocked to the side.

I decided she'd been a good friend so far and I needed to tell *someone*.

"Well, it's just that something happened last night. Something was stolen from my room."

"Stolen?"

"Yes," I took a deep breath. "The only clue I found were boot prints next to my window. With a star in the center. Just like yours."

"So you think I stole it?"

Her eyes narrowed slightly, and she placed her hands on her hips.

"No... I mean it crossed my mind," heat crept up the side of my cheeks. "But I know you would never do that."

Aly dropped her hands to her sides and smiled. "Actually, it *was* me. I came by last night to see if you were awake. But when I tapped the window, you did not respond, so I left. I did not steal anything."

"Right."

Of course, it wasn't Aly. What was I thinking?

"So what was it?" she asked.

I sighed. "It's a long story. I was—"

Aly held her finger up. "Save that thought. I have the perfect spot where you can tell me all about it," she said smiling. Her smile softened the knot in my stomach. "Are you in?" She held out her hand, pinky extended.

"I'm in," I said, hooking her pinky with mine.

"Alright then. Follow me."

Aly turned and started walking through the dark, in the general direction of the museum. Howler monkeys called in the distance and giant bugs chirped in the trees.

I hesitated.

A secret rendezvous in the middle of the night? In the jungle?

It sounded like fun, but there was a part of me that preferred to be under the warm covers of my bed.

Still, Aly was my new best friend, so I could trust her.

Right?

CHAPTER 8
HIDEOUT IN THE JUNGLE

I followed closely on Aly's heels as she led the way through the dark. We'd been walking for several minutes, and the farther we got from the village, the more my palms began to sweat. We stayed on the path, but the surrounding jungle was teeming with strange noises. Screams, caws, and sounds like wild animals came from around every corner, tree, and bush.

We rounded the edge of the Tikal Museum, which I knew to be about a three-minute walk from our cottage and made our way towards the jungle. I hesitated. We were not seriously going into the jungle at night, were we?

Aly stopped and looked back at me. "What is it?"

"Are we going into the jungle?"

Aly nodded. "Just for a bit. Don't worry, I go here all the time."

"Are you sure?"

"Trust me, Harley. You'll love it."

Dad was pretty cool about what he let me do, but going into the jungle at night in a foreign country was not something he'd be on board with. But I also didn't want Aly to think I was some scaredy-cat. I could do this. I could totally do this.

I tried to give her a smile to reassure her I was on board, but every single alarm bell in my mind was going off.

She wouldn't be leading me into a trap, would she?

Just before we were about to step into the jungle, I noticed a strange lightning bolt in the sky. There were no clouds, the air didn't feel damp like it does before a storm, and there was no thunder.

"Aly, do you see that?"

She stopped in front of me and turned her face towards the sky.

"The lightning?"

"Yes," I said. "But there is no storm."

"It must be heat-lightning," she said, shrugging her shoulders.

"What's that?"

"It's just lightning from a distant thunderstorm, that you cannot see or hear. I saw it once before when I was very little."

"Strange," I said. I stared up at it for another moment. It was eerie, seeing the lightning but hearing no sounds.

It gave me a weird feeling.

Aly turned back towards the jungle, gesturing for me to follow. She stepped closer to the thick brush and pushed away a large bush that seemed to be detached from the rest of the foliage.

Once the brush cleared, a thin path emerged in front of us, leading into the jungle. Aly stepped forward without hesitation, beckoning for me to follow. I took one last look toward the museum and followed.

I hope I'm not making the biggest mistake of my short life.

We walked for another thirty seconds, Aly's flashlight bobbing along the path in front of us. Lizards and even a snake scurried out of our path. The jungle air was heavy with rain and my T-shirt clung to my back from a mixture of water and sweat. This was the worst idea I'd ever had. But if I turned back now, would it be even worse? I couldn't leave Aly here, in the jungle alone, and I couldn't walk back home alone either.

"Almost there," said Aly, probably sensing my nervous energy.

She slowed down and stopped. I couldn't really see anything around us except for the thick brush and what appeared to be a giant tree trunk. Aly turned back to me. "Hold this," she said as she handed me her flashlight.

I held the light in my shaking hands as she plunged her hand into her cargo shorts pocket and pulled out a pack of matches. With one strike, she lit the match and then bent down to the tree's giant root system.

Light burst from two metal lamps. More objects took shape in the flickering shadows. Aly reached up and pulled on a rope. A small ladder rolled down the side of the tree trunk. She climbed up into the dark tree. A few moments later, she lit more lamps, and what I saw next nearly took my breath away.

It was a giant treehouse.

"Wow!" I exclaimed as everything came into view. The tree itself had a massive trunk with huge roots that wound around the base like a group of giant snakes. The rope ladder stretched up to meet a wooden platform. The sides of the treehouse were built from a collection of boards, their faded paint still colorful. Corners and edges peaked out from the limbs of the tree, which suggested the thing was huge. I was just seeing the tip of the iceberg.

"Well, what do you think?" Aly asked.

What did I think? I thought it was about the coolest thing I'd ever seen in my life. Definitely worth walking through the jungle in the middle of the night. "It's amazing!"

"Right?" Aly said.

"Right." I eyed the ladder.

"Don't just stand there. Climb on up!" Aly said as she shook the ladder. I hesitated, staring up at her as tiny beads of sweat began to form on my nose.

Did I mention I am *slightly* afraid of heights?

When I was about four years old, my parents thought I would enjoy a hot-air balloon ride over the Grand Canyon. Little did they know, a windstorm would kick us off course and force us to make an emergency landing on the ledge of a deep canyon. I don't remember all of it, but I do remember looking down and thinking how close we were to toppling over the side. I'd been terrified of heights ever since.

Aly was staring at me with an expectant look on her face. I took a deep breath. Did a couple of those calming breaths. They didn't calm me. But I didn't really have a choice.

Here goes nothing.

I turned off the flashlight and tucked it into my backpack and grabbed hold of the sides. The rope ladder creaked and pulled as I shifted my weight. My heart was pounding so loudly I thought even the monkeys could hear it over their own howling. I chanted to myself as I went, *don't look down, don't look down.*

My legs were shaking when I finally reached the top. But I'd done it. Aly stepped inside the arched entryway and waited for me. I gratefully pulled myself into the room, feeling the floor securely beneath me. What I didn't do was turn around and look down.

The main room had a flat roof and was large enough to hold both of us and a collection of supplies. A metal lockbox sat in the corner, along with all sorts of painted jars, a stack of books, and some arrowheads. On the far corner of the room was another ladder, which led up to another platform about six feet above us.

Aly beamed as I took in all the details of the room. "Aly, this is great," I managed to say.

"My brother found it last year when we were on summer break. We have no idea who it used to belong to, but nobody else has come by. So we fixed it up and added a few more features."

"Is it safe?" I tested a few floorboards as I spoke, which creaked in response.

"Totally safe," said Aly, "We have put it to the test." As if to prove her point, she began jumping in place. The floored rocked slightly but held. I raised my hand, signaling her to stop.

"Okay, okay! I believe you."

Aly led me around the rest of the room, showing me her collection of arrowheads and the snacks she had stashed in the metal chest. The treehouse was amazing. Having something like this nearby to where I lived would be the coolest thing ever. Actually, having somewhere I "lived" on a regular basis would be pretty cool. Aly had it all.

She pulled a few objects out of the chest and handed one to me.

"Did you know that the Mayans invented chocolate?" Aly asked.

"Really?"

"Yeah, pretty cool."

She handed me a Crispin chocolate bar. I took a bite, and delicious flavor filled my mouth. Thank you, Mayans! Chocolate was and will always be my favorite treat ever. After I'd gotten through half the bar, I finally got around to what I wanted to tell her. Needed to tell her.

"Remember what I said earlier?" I asked, wiping chocolate from the corners of my mouth.

"You mentioned something was stolen from your room."

I swallowed a crunchy bit of chocolate. "Right. Yesterday I took Daisy out. We walked around the edge of the jungle, and she took off running. We came to a wall made of stacked stones in different shapes, like a game of Tetris. I noticed that there were six small nooks in the wall, five of which had a carved stone sitting inside. But the sixth..."

I paused, peeling the wrapper away from the second half of the chocolate bar. I explained how I recognized the five symbols along the wall: Jaguar, Sun, Snake, Rain, and Skull. And how they were related to each other, representing the Mayan gods. But the sixth nook was empty. And then I found the stone with the glyph for Earth.

"When I placed the stone inside, the ground shook, and there was a little earthquake."

"I felt it too!" said Aly between mouthfuls of chocolate.

"When it was over, I found a little statuette, about a foot long. It was green and looked like it was made out of jade. I had no idea what it was until Dad was talking at dinner about the statues. And that's when I knew. It had to be one of them."

Aly sucked in a breath and raised her hand to her mouth. "Like one of the three Mayan kings?" Her eyes were wide.

"Yes." Relief flooded through me now that it was out. I should have told someone right away, but I hadn't. At least now, I didn't have to carry around the secret on my own. "I picked it up and put it in my backpack. I thought if I did a little research and showed Dad what I found..." I debated telling Aly about how overprotective Dad is, "... he'd be really impressed. So I came to see you first. I was going to have you help me research the statue."

"Oh, right, when I was playing outside with Nacho."

"Exactly. But then, that boy Deacon showed up. So I went home, wrapped the statue in a T-shirt, and hid it under my bed. When we ate dinner in the kitchen that night, Dad told me about the Three Kings. That's when I knew I had to tell him. I hurried back to my room to get the statue. But, when I looked under my bed, it was gone."

Aly was staring at me. "Oh no, Harley, that's terrible. Who do you think stole the statue?"

"I have no idea. I've been looking for clues, but..."

Just as I was about to tell her I was out of ideas, I remembered something in my backpack.

The drawing of the king from the dig site.

CHAPTER 9

A STORM IS BREWING

"Wait." I leapt up and scrambled towards my backpack. It was propped up on the far side of the treehouse where I had dropped it while Aly was giving me a tour. "I have something I need to show you."

I sat across from Aly, crisscrossed my legs, and retrieved the note. I had pulled it out and looked at it several times that day, but nothing made sense.

Maybe Aly would have a better idea of what it was.

She watched as I carefully unfolded the paper and flattened it out in front of her.

"I found this today while we were at the dig site. It looks just like the green statue I found."

"Hmm," Aly said as we stared at the page together. The paper had been folded into four sections. At the top left was a rough sketch of one of the kings. The rest of the page was blank, except for two letters scrawled across the bottom.

C.M.

After a minute or so of staring at

the page, I sighed. "Not much of a clue, I guess."

Aly picked up the page and held it in front of her flashlight. She flipped the page around, studying the back as well.

"It seems like a weird coincidence that it was left at the dig site. And the initials at the bottom..." she bit her lip, twisting the paper in the light. She returned the note to the floor in front of us and wrinkled her nose, deep in thought.

"Do you know a C.M.?" I asked after nearly a minute had gone by.

"Sorry, Harley, I have nada."

"It seems odd that the note has been signed at the bottom, but the middle part is blank..." I brushed some of my hair out of my face, which had sprung a bunch of new curls in the humid air. "Unless..."

"Unless what?" Aly said, staring at me.

"Unless the message is hidden." An idea sprung into my head. "Aly, do you happen to have a black light?"

"I do, but what would you—" she stopped mid-sentence, her eyes lighting up. "Of course! Invisible ink!"

Aly leaped up from her seat and that's when I noticed a huge black shape moving across the room. It had eight hairy legs that spread out from its body and were slowly moving toward Aly's back.

"Look out!" I squeaked as I jumped from my seated position and fled to the other side of the room. Aly bolted towards me, and the two of us tumbled into a heap of supplies propped up in the room's corner.

Aly looked back at where we had been sitting. As I held my breath, I saw the biggest spider I have ever seen walk slowly to the other side of the room. Aly sighed, her body sliding back down to the floor.

Just as I was about to grab a book to swat it with, I heard her start to giggle.

"Oh, Harley, it's just a little tarantula. People keep them as pets around here."

My cheeks filled with heat. "But, what if it—"

"They are not poisonous. The big fangs scare most people, but they rarely bite," she shook her head as she spoke, a small smirk at the edge of her lips. "You should have seen the look on your face."

She burst out laughing again, which turned out to be contagious. Pretty soon, both of us were rolling on the floor in a fit of giggles... Although I still kept my distance from the spider.

After a few moments, the spider scuttled away. I looked around to be sure it was gone. We had knocked an entire stack of journals, books and writing utensils to the floor.

"Here, let me help you clean this up," I said.

"My black light pen should be in here somewhere. My mom got it for me as a gift, so I could keep a journal without Ricardo reading it."

I wondered what it was like to have a brother as we rifled through the pens, markers, and pencils that were scattered on the floor.

"Found it! Harley, where is that note?"

In all the commotion, the note had been kicked across the room. We spotted it at the same time. Aly ran over, picked it up, and brought it back to the center of the room. She flattened it out on the floor and I positioned the black light just over the top.

As soon as I did, the words appeared.

If you want your little statue back, meet me
On Wednesday at the Temple of the Jaguar.
2pm sharp.
Don't be late.–C.M.

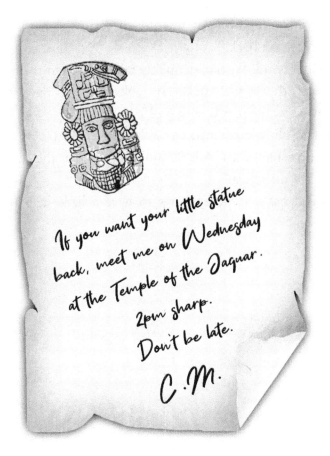

"A clue!" we both shouted.

A meeting at the Temple of the Jaguar. That was at the dig site! I knew just where it was. But who was C.M.? And who was this note intended for?

"Wednesday, that's tomorrow," I could feel the butterflies

bouncing around in my stomach as I spoke. "We need to be there. Find out who C.M. is and get back that statue!"

Aly nodded. I was about to launch into all my doubts and questions when I heard an ominous clap of thunder. Aly and I both looked up.

"A storm is coming." Aly was already getting to her feet. "Come on, we have to get back."

"Right," I said. We had definitely taken a step in the right direction to get the statue back. "It looks like we have a meeting tomorrow at two. Are you with me?"

Aly had already reached the ladder and was facing me as she took the first step down. A little smile appeared at the corner of her mouth. "Yes, mi amiga."

I smiled back. It never hurts to have a little help from your friends.

CHAPTER 10

THE BELLY OF THE BEAST

"All done!" I cried, slamming my science textbook shut. Jessica looked up at me, startled. It was one-thirty already. I had barely been able to focus on my homework. All I could think about was the meeting. And who C.M. was.

"That was fast. You in a hurry to go somewhere?"

"Yes, I'm meeting Aly over at the museum," I stood up from the kitchen table and searched the room for my backpack. It was drizzling rain outside, so we'd done my tutoring inside. "If that's okay with you? We're gonna do some research."

Jessica gave me a knowing smile. "Research?"

"Well, yeah. And hang out. And…"

Okay, it was a bit of a white lie. I felt a twinge of guilt. But once we got that statue back…

"It's fine," Jessica said. "What time will you be back?"

"Probably for dinner." I slung my backpack over my shoulder and headed for the door.

"Have fun. And don't forget your rain jacket."

I grabbed my yellow rain jacket with a nod of thanks and then made my way down the path.

Aly and I had made plans to meet at the museum and then head over to the Temple of the Jaguar, one of the main attractions in Tikal. There was a gravel path that connected the village where I was staying to the museum. I trudged along, thankful for my waterproof boots.

The jungle took on another personality when it rained. The birds and animals quieted, the steady rainfall rocking them to sleep like a lullaby. Tourists were few and far between, probably waiting for the weather to deliver a clear day. A mist clung to the air just above me, which made the entire site feel a bit mysterious.

It wasn't until I was just a few yards away from the museum that I saw Aly emerge from the back wearing a blue rain jacket. She raised her arm and waved me over.

"Are you ready?" I was a bit breathless, my heart racing inside my chest as I approached her.

"Totally," said Aly, a flash of excitement in her eyes. "I have collected all the supplies we need."

Aly had borrowed a set of headlamps, a length of rope, and two walkie-talkies from the museum supply cabinet. I had snacks and water. We were prepared for adventure; although, I had no idea what that adventure would look like.

We walked side by side through the light fog. The clouds had blocked out much of the sunlight, and even though it was only mid-afternoon, it was definitely dark. I let Aly take the lead since she knew her way around the buildings of Tikal much better than I did.

"You know the Jaguar was the ruler of the underworld," Aly said. "This temple is nine levels high, which represents the nine levels of the underworld."

"Like the underworld from Greek mythology?" I asked.

"Yes! Where you would go after you die. Except the Mayans

called it Xibalba," Aly's eyes twinkled slightly as she continued. She did her best deep voice. "Which means 'Place of Fear.'"

A shiver slid up my sides as if my body were warning me of something. *The place of fear is right.*

Before I could have any more second thoughts, we broke through the edge of the jungle path and emerged behind the temple itself. I looked up at the structure, which towered a hundred feet above us, breaking through the fog that hung Tikal.

The gloom might actually work to our advantage. Our brightly colored rain jackets provided little secrecy.

"What if they see us? The people who have the statue?" Aly whispered.

I shrugged, "We'll just pretend we're tourists and walk away."

As we stepped toward the temple, a light came from an opening near the base of the steps. *That's odd.*

I didn't know there was a way in. I stopped and nudged Aly with my elbow and pointed. She narrowed her eyes and leaned her head forward.

"I've never noticed that before," she said, wiping a bit of rain from her forehead.

My eyes scanned the area, but nobody was nearby. We continued walking towards the light.

When we reached the temple, the light was gone. But behind a thick cluster of vines was a doorway. The vines looked as if they had been recently moved.

Aly pulled the headlamps out of her backpack, and we put them on. As we flicked our beams upward, a long dark hallway illuminated before us. There were stacked stones lining the sides and spiderwebs crisscrossing the ceiling, which was about eight feet high. I shivered when I spotted the large webs.

I touched Aly's arm. "Are you sure about this?"

"Don't worry, Harley. I have been playing around these temples since I was little," she said, giving me a small smile. "What is the worst that could happen?"

I had no intention of answering that question.

I stepped in behind her.

The air was much cooler inside. I focused on putting one foot in front of the other, and before I knew it, the doorway shrank in the distance behind us. The space was *tight*. Aly and I exchanged looks, and for a moment, I thought we might both be ready to turn back.

I took a deep breath and pushed forward. A few seconds later, I saw a large cavern open up several more feet to the ceiling.

"Look," I whispered, pointing my light into the darkness in front of us. "Up ahead is an open chamber."

We stepped inside. Our headlamps bounced off the walls, which were painted with colorful artwork, showing snakes, people with the heads of jaguars, and more.

"I have never seen *this* before," Aly said under her breath.

"It's amazing," I replied, the light from my headlamp moving around the room. For a few moments, we were lost in the dazzling display of colors and architecture. Walls were covered in swirls of turquoise and blue, with painted Mayans giving gifts to their gods. In another scene, Mayan people were wrapped in flames while serpents and monkeys towered over their heads.

Then the sounds of footsteps approaching from the far side of the chamber startled us back to the present.

"Quick, over here," I said. "Aly, your light!"

She reached up and flicked off her headlamp, and we were suddenly plunged into total darkness. I grabbed Aly's arm and pulled her behind something, probably one of the large pillars. The footsteps grew closer. Sweat crept down my back and under my arms.

As the noise grew louder, a flickering light filled the room.

They were going to find us. Even if they couldn't see us, surely they would be able to hear the sound of my heart beating in my chest. It was so loud in my ears I thought it might pop right out.

From what I could tell, there were three sets of feet shuffling through the chamber behind us. I held my breath. The seconds slogged on for what felt like hours. My legs started cramping. Dust built up in my throat. I couldn't last any longer.

Then I heard the voices, just a few feet from us.

"You don't know what you're doing. That statue—"

British accent. That must be —

"Listen, kid. We don't believe in the legends. That statue is worth more money than you can possibly understand."

"Oh, I understand. And I won't—"

The voices bounced off the walls and were lost down the hall-way. The sounds of footsteps faded. Aly and I both exhaled.

"I think they're gone," I said, keeping my voice low and holding in the cough that threatened to break free.

"I think you are right," Aly said, flicking her light back on. I did the same.

"That was close."

"Who do you think that was?" she asked.

My headlamp lit up Aly's face. She had been sweating as well. I was glad I wasn't the only one who was nearly scared out of my boots.

"I don't know who the men were. But I'm certain that was Deacon."

"The British boy from the museum?"

"Yes," I answered. "We can talk more later, right now I just want to get out of here."

Aly nodded and stepped back toward the hallway we had walked in through. I was just about to turn that way myself when my light landed on something sitting on the floor.

"Aly, wait," I said as I knelt down. "Look."

She turned back and dropped to a knee at my side. I shone my light on the small object from the floor.

It was a small gold medallion on a leather rope. I looked closer. It was engraved with an owl, a half-moon crown, and it was ringed by words. Society of Mystical Artifacts, Legends, and Lore.

I stared at the object in my hand. I knew who this belonged to... Deacon.

"Look, this is his. Now I know it's him."

Aly stopped and looked back at me. "You know he will want that back," she said.

"I'm counting on it," I replied with a smile playing on my lips. An idea was forming in my head. A way for us to get that statue back where it belonged.

Just as I was about to share my plan with Aly, a loud bang shook the hallway. Dust shifted in the air, and the sound of the drizzling rain outside disappeared.

"What was that?" I turned to Aly, my eyes wide. But I already knew the answer.

That was the door.

We had just been shut inside the Temple of the Grand Jaguar.

CHAPTER 11
WHEN ONE DOOR CLOSES...

We ran back down the hall to the entrance of the temple. It was just as I had feared.

The sound had been the door closing. The large stone entrance was shut as solid as a tomb. Whoever had moved past us in the chamber had walked outside and closed the door behind them.

Whether they knew it or not, they had locked us inside.

We shoved and pushed on the door as sweat dripped down every inch of my body. But the thing wouldn't move. We were trapped.

"It's stuck," I told Aly as we took a breather, leaning up against the wall of the temple.

I tried not to panic. When I was about seven years old, my parents were working in a dig site near Cairo in Egypt. I had stepped away from them, just for a moment to explore a nearby tomb. I was just a few feet into a dark, narrow hallway when a couple stones broke loose near the entrance. I'd been trapped. It took an hour to dig me out.

Ever since then, I had dreaded small spaces. This current situation wasn't exactly helping calm my fears.

Breathe, Harley.

We had flipped our headlamps back on, using the sliver of light to guide us. I tried my cell phone, but the thick stone walls blocked out any chance for a cell signal.

"You know this place, right?" I asked as calm as possible. "Are there any other ways out?"

I pulled out some water and handed it to Aly. She took a drink and shook her head from side to side.

"I did not know this chamber was even in here," she said, handing the bottle back to me.

"When those people passed us in the chamber, they came from the other direction. Maybe there's another way into the temple."

Aly gave the door one last shove before responding. "Let's hope so because I don't think this door is going to budge."

We walked single file, me in front and Aly trailing behind. With the door closed, the air felt thicker and heavier. Or maybe it was my paranoid imagination. Still, I worried about the oxygen supply as we headed deeper into the belly of the Jaguar.

When we arrived back at the chamber, instead of studying the paintings on the wall, we searched the room for another way out. The room was way bigger than I had originally thought. It was in the shape of a rectangle, and it seemed to stretch forward about twenty feet into the darkness. As Aly and I headed towards the opposite end of the room, the eyes in the paintings seemed to watch us as we passed.

Creepy.

"Aly, look, it's a doorway," I said, pointing both her hand and her light towards a dark rectangle at the end of the hall.

We picked up our pace, anxious for a possible way out. As the light from our headlamps illuminated the space, we both realized what it was at the same time.

"Stairs!" we exclaimed in unison. "Jinx!"

We laughed a welcome change from the fear gripping my chest. "Where do you think it goes?" Aly asked.

"My guess? The door at the top of the temple," I said as she peered into the passageway, looking up. "At least, I hope."

I remembered the small door at the point of the pyramid from my frequent walks with Daisy around Tikal. I often wondered where it led, but tourists were no longer allowed to walk up the temple steps. Dad had said it was too dangerous to climb the stairs, so the little door remained a mystery.

But given our current situation? I figured Dad would prefer I try the stairs instead of being stuck in here.

"Alright." I swallowed. "Let's go."

I followed Aly up the ancient stone staircase. The space was so narrow I could touch both walls as I climbed. Step by step, we made our way up the nine levels of the temple. Around the fifth level, my mind started to wander. The medallion I'd found...it was Deacon's! I'd seen him wearing it the first time we met.

How was he involved in this whole thing? He seemed friendly and not friendly all at the same time. It wasn't too difficult to imagine that he had something to do with this missing statue. Was he at the meeting today? And if so, was he there to get the statue back, or had he stolen it?

The note had been signed *C.M.* I tried to think of anyone I knew with those initials, but nothing came to mind.

"Water break?" Aly called from ahead of me. I stopped, pulled the two bottles of water out of my backpack, and handed one to her.

"So why do you think that Deacon boy was here in the temple?" she asked as we huddled together in the dark.

"I don't know," I said between gulps. Nine flights were a lot of stairs. "But he must have something to do with the note...and the statue."

Aly cocked her head as if considering this. "He did seem a little odd. Like—"

"Like he was hiding something?" I said.

"Exactly." She looked up the stairs. "Well, if we get out of here—"

"Not if. When. Because we are totally getting out of here." I gave her my bravest smile. "We just have to find a way. Let's go."

I hoped I was right.

I turned and continued to climb. After another five minutes or so, we reached a platform area. Just like the chamber below, it was painted with Mayan artwork; gods, slaves, animals. Aly and I couldn't help but let our eyes sweep around the room. It was stuff like this that made me understand Dad's fascination.

"It's hard to believe this was all painted thousands of years ago," I said, newfound respect blooming for the ancient Mayan people. People today had no idea of the artistry, scientific thought, and genius of some of these civilizations. The Mayans revolutionized astronomy, created a calendar, and designed musical instruments that were far ahead of their time.

"Right? Since I grew up around these ruins, sometimes I take it for granted."

"Hey, look here," I said, pointing my light to a collection of paintings. "That looks like the statues of the Three Kings."

The statues were painted in bright colors, with swirls of green wrapped around them. I recognized the one I had found in the jungle, sitting in the middle. In the next scene, the kings had emerged out of their statues and into their human forms. They looked angry. Standing behind them were thousands of soldiers with heads made of skulls and red glowing eyes. They carried spears.

"I have never seen paintings of the three statues actually," said

Aly, stepping closer. "I thought the legend only existed as a campfire story."

I ran my hands over the cool stone. I could feel the ripples of paint under my fingertips. "What's this?" I pointed to a couple of symbols at the bottom.

"That's a Mayan calendar date. It represents the Baktun."

"Let me guess...the thirteenth Baktun," I said as a shiver ran up my spine.

"I think so," said Aly.

"We better get out of here. Because if this legend is real..." I didn't have the courage to say the words out loud.

My eyes swept the room. I noticed a small crack of light on the west wall of the room.

"Is that a door?"

Aly didn't respond but made her way towards the light. I followed. Unlike the rest of the temple, the door was made of rough wood. Probably added in later to keep the looters out. Light filtered through a gap that was only a few inches wide. Just enough to get my fingers around it.

"Let's push it together," I said, squeezing my hands in the gap. Aly placed her fingers just below mine, and we tried to slide the door to the side.

The door moved! Okay, it barely budged, but that was something. There was hope.

"Let's try it again," I said. "On three. One, two, three..."

We both grabbed hold of the door's edge and heaved.

It opened!

Okay, open may be stretching it a bit. It was cracked about a foot, but it should be enough for us to fit. I could hear the rainfall outside again and taste the fresh air.

We were close.

Aly and I stripped off our backpacks and squirmed through one at a time. Once we stepped outside, a rush of relief swept over my body. I leaned heavily on the stone wall behind me.

We were on a small landing area with a stone slab hanging over our heads. It was about four feet by four feet. Aly made her way towards the edge of the landing and looked down.

I pushed myself off the wall and walked towards her. As I stepped up to her side, I kicked a small stone sitting on the edge of the landing. It launched off the side of the temple and tumbled down the steep stone. I stood there watching it fall—all one hundred and fifty feet to the ground.

"Whoa." My whole body swayed. I could already feel my head growing light. I stumbled back towards the doorway, slipping on the wet stones.

Although we had found our way out of the temple, we now had a new problem. A steep one.

How in the world were we going to make it down the side of this gigantic temple on a pile of wet, stone steps?

CHAPTER 12

DON'T LOOK DOWN

"I don't think I can do it," I told Aly as I stood clinging to the side of the temple. Staring at the rows of slick steps that swept down the side of the building made me want to throw up. Aly might as well have been asking me to jump off the edge of the Grand Canyon.

"Come on, Harley, I know you can. I have done this before."

"But the steps, they're wet, what if..."

Aly walked back toward me and took me by the arms, looking into my eyes. "Do you have a better idea?"

My mind went into super-speed, trying to come up with a solution. I pictured the temple in 3D, twirling like a triangular top in my head.

That's when an idea hit me.

The nine levels of the Temple of the Jaguar. Still steep, still scary. But it was better than sliding down those slippery front steps.

The Maya believed that when you died, you must pass through these nine levels to reach the afterlife; hence, the reason for the temple terraces we were standing on. From the place for crossing the water to the place of obsidian, each level had a special meaning.

I gulped. I definitely wasn't ready to drop down to the underworld. But we didn't have much of a choice.

"The nine levels," I said, swirls of anxiety bouncing around my stomach.

"You mean—"

"The nine terraces that run down the side of the temple. They aren't as slippery, and we can drop down them one at a time."

Aly stared at me with her big brown eyes. She cocked her head to one side. I couldn't tell what she would say next. Then she smiled.

"You're sure?"

I tried to form a smile in return, although the rising fear in my stomach held me back.

"Trust me, it's a much easier way to go," I said, trying to sound confident. "Plus, if we go down the front steps and get caught, we will both be in big trouble."

She knew I was right. Dad would kill me if he saw me trying to go down the steps of the temple. What little freedom I had would vanish.

I looked over Aly's shoulder at the terraces. I could do this... I hoped. Not like I had much of a choice.

"Okay," she said finally, taking a deep breath.

Aly and I made our way out of the little entry area and to the first terrace. I practically hugged the walls as we moved across the temple's back side. I took one glance down the side of the building.

Huge mistake.

The sight of the long drop sent a wave of pins and needles through my body.

"Oh, no—" I said, stumbling on a broken piece of stone. My head spun, and I felt a sickening weightlessness like I was about to fall. Just when I thought I might tumble down the side of this big stone pyramid, Aly grabbed my arm.

"I got you," she said, pulling me back to the wall. "From now on, focus on me, okay?"

I nodded. It was the second time in twenty-four hours my fear of heights had been tested. Aly was my friend, don't get me wrong, but I'd have preferred it if we hung out on the ground more often.

We set our sights on dropping down the first terrace. Each section was about fifteen feet. But unlike the steps, there was plenty of room to stand, sit, and lay down on each landing. Making it much less of a fall risk.

At least, I hoped.

Aly approached our first drop. She slid her body over the side, and just when her fingers hit the edge of the terrace, she let go. I peered over the side to see if she had made it. She was standing down below.

"Nothing to it!" she called up to me. "Your turn, amiga!"

She made it look so easy.

While Aly slid over the edge and dropped down in about thirty seconds, it took me a bit longer. More like ten minutes. Aly coached me along the whole way, and when I finally reached the edge, it felt like my body just refused to let go.

"Come on, Harley, you got this!"

Sweat covered every bit of my body. My hair was stuck to the sides of my face from the rain, and the contents of my lunch were slowly making their way up my throat. But eventually, I closed my eyes and let go. I opened them just in time to hit the terrace.

As I crouched down on the wide landing, Aly slapped me on the back. "You did it!"

"I did!" I almost cried. I was so relieved.

That wasn't so bad, right?

Aly was already making her way to the edge of the next drop. "Only eight more drops to go!"

Oh boy.

It took us another thirty minutes to drop down the rest of the way, but we finally hit the jungle floor. I was so exhausted from the adrenaline I could have laid on the ground and gone to sleep right then and there. During our climb, the rain clouds had cleared away, and a few rays of sunshine were poking through the trees. The sun had begun its descent towards the earth.

"We better get back," I said.

"Right, but what about the medallion?" Aly asked. "Why would Deacon's necklace have been here of all places, right when we were?"

I hooked my thumbs into the straps of my backpack, looking back towards the village.

"Why don't we go ask him?"

CHAPTER 13
A CHANGE OF PLANS

The sensation of falling was different from what I had imagined. The breeze curled around my body as it rushed toward the ground. My arms and legs swung through the air, trying to find something, anything, to grab onto.

A scream was lodged in my throat, but I couldn't open my mouth to let it out. The ground below me was getting closer, the blades of grass rushing at me. I knew if I hit the ground, it would be over.

As I pulled my arms in front of me to soften the fall, I saw it. The small glowing jade statue. I finally opened my mouth to scream.

"Harley!" Jessica's voice shocked me out of my sleep.

I sat up in bed, the sheets sticking to me from a nervous sweat. It had been a dream. Better yet, a nightmare. I had tossed and turned all night, barely able to get any sleep.

What time is it?

"Coming, Jessica," I yelled as I stumbled out of bed. The sun was peeking through my window. I had probably missed Dad before he left for the day. Jessica was waiting in the kitchen, along with a bowl of oatmeal and orange juice.

"Sleep okay?" she asked as her eyes surveyed my tired face.

"Not really," I said. If I told Jessica what happened yesterday at the temple, she'd flip out and tell Dad, and I'd never be able to leave the house again. "The storm kept me up."

"Aw, I see." She took a sip of her coffee. "Eat your breakfast and maybe we can take a ride into Flores later and catch a movie."

Movies were my favorite. Having traveled all over the world to remote locations, movies were a luxury I usually had no access to. There was no question. I would love to see a movie.

The problem was I needed to find that statue.

"I'm worried I might fall asleep during a movie."

Daisy padded over to me with a friendly lick of my leg. "Mind if I walk Daisy?"

"Sure," she said as her eyes wandered back over to her laptop. She'd been spending an awful lot of time on it lately—more than usual. "There are some interesting clouds in the sky today; something they haven't seen in a hundred years here."

Interesting clouds? What does that mean?

As soon as I stepped out into the clearing next to our little bungalow, I knew what she meant. Above the jungle in the distance were strange-looking pink clouds that were swirling high above the treetops. It looked like the Mayan gods were making cotton candy in the sky.

I could feel the little hairs on the back of my neck stand up as Daisy pulled me forward.

I would have to ask Jessica about those later. For now, I needed to see Deacon.

My eyes swept over the collection of houses until I spotted the blue cottage where he was staying, and I hurried over and knocked on the front door. No answer. I walked around the back of the cottage and looked for anyone who might be able to help. But there was no one around.

Now what?

Daisy yipped at my side and pulled the leash in my hand.

"May I help you?"

I turned around, startled by the voice. It came from a woman with a distinct British accent, just like Deacon's.

"Um, yes, I was looking for Deacon?"

The woman smiled at me, her pale blue eyes twinkling in the morning sun. She had fair skin and strawberry blonde hair. She reminded me a little of my mother.

"Deacon is doing the zip line today," she said.

"Zip line?"

"Yes, at the Tikal Canopy Tour just north of here."

I knew what the canopy tour was. It was an obstacle course high up in the trees with suspended platforms, ropes, and zip lines. I gulped.

No way was I ever doing anything like that.

"Okay, thanks!"

I turned and walked as quickly as I could back to our cottage. I had to talk to Deacon today. If I waited until Dad came home from the dig, I would miss my chance. Dad insists we sit down for dinner together. No escaping from that.

But how in the world was I going to get answers from Deacon if he was zipping through the jungle treetops?

The answer, of course, was simple.

I needed to convince Jessica that instead of a movie, we should go on a zip line adventure.

As Daisy trotted along in front of me, I tried to think of an angle where Jessica wouldn't suspect my true motive.

Because why in the world would Harley James, the girl who was terrified of heights, ask to go on a zip line tour?

"I'm trying to get over my fear of heights," I said confidently a few minutes later. Jessica and I stood in the cottage kitchen. I studied her face and waited for her reaction.

Jessica shrugged. "Sounds good to me. Let me check with your dad first."

That was much easier than I thought. I almost wished she'd said no.

I went to my room to get changed and pack my backpack. If only I could pack some courage, everything would be great. But courage was nowhere to be found.

I was just about ready to walk back into the kitchen and call the whole thing off when Jessica popped her head into the room.

"Your dad is fine with it," she said, giving my outfit of shorts and a teal #DogLife T-shirt a once over. "I have a friend who is a tour guide there, so we can get in for free. We leave in five minutes. Don't forget your bug spray."

My stomach did a triple flip as I imagined myself screeching across the jungle canopy on a tiny wire. Daisy was panting at my feet. I reached down to scratch the center of her furry forehead.

I hope this little statue is worth it.

CHAPTER 14

TREETOPS ARE FOR BIRDS

"One, two, three.... Go!"

The ever-patient zip line tour guide was shouting instructions at me for the third time. I wasn't about to budge. I stood on top of a platform, approximately one hundred and forty feet in the air. I had all the trappings of an adventurous zip liner: hard hat, harness, gloves. But inside, my nerves were strung tight like guitar strings.

"Senorita, if you don't jump, I'm going to have to push you, or you must climb back down."

I looked below me, my hands wrapping tightly around the rope with a white-knuckled grip. Climbing back down the rickety rope ladder wasn't a more appealing option. At least the other end of the zip line was *lower* than my current location.

Sweat now leaked out of my body and formed dark rings around the neck and arms of my cotton T-shirt. I puffed a bit of air, trying to blow the wet strands of hair off my forehead.

I could totally do this, right?

Before our climb, the tour guide had informed me that in the ten years since Tikal Canopy Tours had started, they had zero fatalities. I suppose that should make me feel better. But as I stared down at the jungle brush below, all I could think of was *there's a first for everything.*

Jessica was waiting on the other side of the platform for me, waving her arms and giving me the thumbs up. There was also another person off in the distance who caught my attention. The pale skin and carrot-colored hair were hard to miss.

Deacon.

I spotted him as soon as we arrived about thirty minutes ago. He was with a small group of local kids, a few platforms ahead of us. I rushed Jessica through the paperwork to get started on the tour, and we managed to snag a spot just one group behind Deacon's. I figured if we could finish about the same time as him and his friends, or just after, I could confront him about the statue.

I felt the small bulge of his gold owl engraved medallion in my backpack. I studied the object this morning. It had a travel-worn look to it, which suggested that it had been many places with its owner. Which also meant that Deacon was likely attached to it, giving me just the leverage I needed to extract any information I could about the missing statue.

Or even better, trading it for the missing statue itself.

"One, two—"

The missing statue.

I snapped back to attention and squeezed my eyes closed so tightly that I could practically feel my eyebrows touch my cheeks.

And then, I, Harley James, a girl who was deathly afraid of heights, jumped.

"Whooaaa.....Ahhhh!"

The wind whipped past me as I bulleted through the air. I imagined this is what it felt like to be Superman, except with much less courage. And I believe he flew with his eyes open, which mine currently were not.

"Harley, open your eyes!" I heard Jessica call to me as I rushed through the air.

No way, no how.

I managed to make it to the other end of the line with my eyes shut the entire time. I didn't open them until a pair of hands reached out, grabbed my harness, and pulled me safely to the floor.

"You did it!" Jessica gave me a big smile and a high five. "Way to face your fears, kiddo!"

I smiled back. I didn't have any words at this moment, especially since I was about to lose my breakfast. My insides felt like they had been flipped upside down and wound back together in a knot.

After a few wobbly minutes regaining my composure, I looked to the group ahead of us, which was about thirty feet to our south. I kept my eye on Deacon's group for the rest of the tour, trying in some feeble way to catch up with them.

The entire process was torture. One second, I convinced myself I was no longer afraid of heights. The next minute, I was hurtling through the trees, ready to vomit. But after several grueling trips down the wire, we made it to the end of the tour. Jessica congratulated me on a job well done, but I felt light-headed and weak.

As we reached the end of the tour, I was exhausted. I placed my backpack somewhere safe and used the last bit of my strength to sneak into the edge of the jungle and spy on Deacon. I spotted his group, but I couldn't find him anywhere.

"Excuse me," I said to one guy in his group, "Have you seen Deacon?"

"Sorry, love, he wandered off right after we finished," he replied in a cheerful British accent. "But his backpack's right over there, so I'm sure he'll be back."

My eyes followed to where he was pointing, and there indeed was Deacon's pack. I recognized it from the other day.

"Thanks," I mumbled as I walked towards it. I glanced around me as I stood over his pack, just to make sure no one was looking.

Then I did something that I would never normally do. Something that went against everything Dad had taught me. I grabbed his backpack and searched inside.

I wasn't sure what I was hoping to find, but at this point, I was desperate. I had to find that little statue.

As luck would have it, I found a folded piece of paper inside. I was just about to open it up when I heard the guy from earlier.

"Ello, Deacon, there was a girl looking for you..."

I dropped the backpacked and scrambled back towards Jessica.

I shuffled back to the clearing to stand with the rest of the group.

I was exhausted.

I slid my back down the side of a giant Kapok tree to rest, which was bigger than the bedroom I was staying in. Jessica was chatting with her friend Manuel, the tour guide. She asked me to sit and wait. I began to unfold the small note when a familiar voice startled me.

"Harley?"

I shoved the note in my pocket.

"Hi, Deacon."

He sat down on a stump next to me. He was holding a bottle of water in his hand and took a long drink. Sweat soaked through a bandana he had wrapped around his head.

"I heard you were looking for me?"

Oh no...

"Me? Oh no, I was just out ziplining..." It came out like more of a question than an answer.

"Right, just out ziplining," Deacon chuckled. "Pretty fun, right?"

"Uh-huh," I muttered. Not my idea of fun, but since Deacon was here...

I used what strength I had left and rose to my feet. It was time to confront Deacon. I thrust my hand down in my pocket to retrieve the medallion. I moved my hand around, searching.

The medallion was gone!

Deacon was watching me, his head cocked. "You okay?"

"Yes, I'm fine," I reached my hand over to the other pocket. The note was there, but no medallion. "I think I just lost something."

"Do you need me to help you find—"

"No, no, it's fine." Heat crept up the sides of my cheeks.

Facing my fear of heights tired me so much that I forgot I had placed his medallion in my backpack.

"So, uh," I opened my backpack to search for the medallion. It wasn't there either. "Have you been enjoying Tikal?"

Deacon shrugged. "Yes, it's quite lovely. The wild jungle, the history of the Mayan people, the—"

"The Legend of the Three Kings?" I looked up at him.

Something fluttered across his eyes and he stared at me. "What do you know of the legend?"

"Just that they have found two of the statues. And the third one is *missing*," I emphasized the last word, narrowing my eyes as I spoke.

"I'm sure they'll find it," he replied. He then raised his hand to his open mouth, faking a yawn. "Listen, I'm knackered. Going to head back to the village."

"Are you sure you don't—"

"See you around, Harley James," he turned on his heel and walked back toward his group.

I opened my mouth to ask more questions but decided against

it. Without his little medallion, I didn't have any leverage. I dropped my shoulders. My chance to get some answers out of Deacon, and I blew it.

I felt the note in my pocket. *Or maybe not.*

When Deacon was clearly out of sight, I opened it up. To my surprise, it was an entire page of numbers. I flipped it upside down and held it up to the light.

What was Deacon doing with a page of numbers?

It didn't make any sense.

Jessica was calling my name. It was time to go home. I could feel my stomach growling. Maybe a little food in my stomach would help me figure out what to do next.

But one thing was certain, Deacon was hiding something.

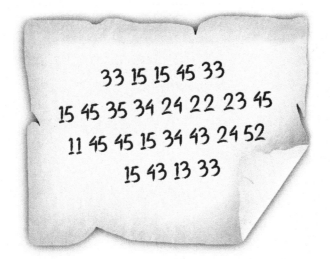

CHAPTER 15
SNEAKIN' DEACON

"Not hungry tonight, Cat-Cat?"

I pushed some beans around the edge of my plate, staring into space. Dad must have caught on to my gloomy outlook. But how could I tell him what was wrong? He would be so disappointed in me.

"I guess not," I said, trying to hide my sour attitude.

"Jessica tells me that you went zip lining in the treetops today. I'm so impressed!"

I smiled despite myself. I actually *was* kind of proud that I faced my fear of heights. Even though I nearly lost my lunch. Also, I'd opened my eyes on the last few rides, and it was pretty freaking amazing.

"It was kind of fun," I said, finally putting a small forkful of beans in my mouth.

"Well, you are one brave girl. I know you don't like heights."

"How was your day, Dad?"

He sat back in his chair and used a napkin to wipe his mouth. He took a deep breath.

"We ran into a problem."

I put my fork down. "What kind of problem?"

"The statues we recovered—the two jade kings—have gone missing."

My heart jumped into my throat. "What?"

"Yes, it's true," he said, a worried look crossing his face. "I was hoping to bring our find to the meeting tomorrow with our sponsors; however, it doesn't look like we'll be able to."

"That's terrible." My heart ached seeing Dad so disappointed.

"It happens. Some people would rather sell these treasures for money than share them with a museum."

I thought of my mom at that moment. The past is sacred. It's our duty to protect what others left behind, she would say.

"I heard about the Legend of the Three Kings. That if they all came together—"

He shook his head.

"That's just a myth, Cat-Cat."

"Mom would have believed it," I said, feeling a sting in my eyes. My mother loved to tell me the myths and legends of any place we visited. I would always ask her if she believed they were true. She would smile back and say, "Maybe one day we will find out."

I sat back in my chair, a wave of sadness and guilt cresting over my body. This situation was all my fault. If only I had given the statue to Dad when I first found it.

For a moment, I thought about spilling the beans and telling him the whole story. But he looked so disappointed, sitting there at the table. I didn't have the heart to deliver more bad news.

"How's the Junior International Cryptography Competition going?"

This lifted my spirits a bit.

"I just solved the riddle for week two."

Dad broke out in a smile. "You are quite the cryptographer."

Cryptography... That's it! The numbers on Deacon's note! It's in code!

"May I be excused? I'm pretty tired," I said, trying to hide my excitement.

"Sure, honey." Dad gave me a kiss on the forehead, and I headed to my room. Daisy followed me in and jumped on my bed as I ripped the note out of my bag.

I stared at the numbers.

33 15 15 45 33 15 45 35 34 24 22 23 45 11 45 45 15 34 43 24 52 15 43 13 33

It was a Polybius square code. I was sure of it. I quickly wrote out the cipher and went to work.

33 15 15 45 33 15 45 35 34
24 22 23 45 11 45 45 15 34
43 24 52 15 43 13 33

POLYBIUS SQUARE

	1	2	3	4	5
1	A	B	C	D	E
2	F	G	H	I	J
3	K	L	M	N	O
4	P	Q	R	S	T
5	U	V	W	X	Y

33=M   15=E

I tracked the numbers, 3 across and 3 down. I wrote down the letter M. Then I went to the next combination, 1 across and 5 down. I wrote down the letter E.

When I was finished, I stared at the words.

"Meet me tonight at ten. River. C.M."

So Deacon is meeting someone. But who? And what river?

I flopped back in my bed, jolting Daisy out of her nap.

"Sorry, girl."

Great, now I'm back to square one.

I laid there for a long time, staring at the ceiling. I should have confronted Deacon about the statue while we were standing under the Kopak tree. I thought about how the conversation might have gone.

Me: Do you know where the missing statue is?

Deacon: Sure, let me grab it from my backpack and give it to you.

Okay, that was not going to happen. So maybe I didn't blow it after all.

But still, Deacon always seemed to pop wherever I found a clue that led to finding the statue..

Sneakin' Deacon.

And now, all three were missing.

I couldn't just sit there. I had to do something. Dad's meeting was coming up. Those statues were not going to find themselves.

I thought about my options, running my hand through Daisy's fur.

The realization came to me. Whoever stole the one statue probably had the other two as well. According to legend, this would give the person immense power or bring about a zombie apocalypse, depending on which legend you believed in.

But with all the strange things that had been happening around Tikal—the earthquake, the cicadas, the strange lightning, and the swirling pink clouds—I was really starting to believe the legend was true.

I had to do something.

If I could just find one statue, I could stop the legendary return of the kings before the final Baktun.

I spotted my laptop in the room's corner. Dad and I shared a cloud storage account where he kept all the photos of his expeditions, and I had kept photos of my own. I popped it open on my bed and went back to the day of the dig. There were about fifty photos to sort through.

I could see Aly, myself, and Ricardo. I saw Dad.

Nothing really stood out.

And then I noticed someone else...

Bingo!

I shut the screen and stashed the laptop in my backpack.

I needed to show this to Aly, pronto.

"Come on, Daisy," I said, gathering my backpack. It was way past my bedtime, but I probably wouldn't sleep anyway.

I walked over and put my ear to my door. Daisy padded over and looked up at me. I could hear Dad and Jessica talking. They were still at the dinner table. Which was good because it meant I could sneak out the window.

I climbed onto the bed tugged at the screen in the window. It took some work, but I was able to shake it loose and prop open the window. I carefully dropped Daisy outside the window first, then climbed out behind her.

The sun had dropped into the jungle, its job was done for the day, and the moon was casting long shadows through the jungle trees. Daisy and I hustled over to Aly's house. I figured I'd tap on her window this time.

But I didn't have to. She was out with Nacho.

Daisy began tugging at her leash to get over to her pal. But then I noticed something and held her back.

The fading light cast a lot of shadows. Despite Daisy's eagerness, Aly still hadn't seen me. And she was not alone.

She stood next to a man wearing a broad-brimmed hat. It didn't look like the jungle helmets so common in Guatemala. Or one of the soft bucket hats that a lot of people wore to keep the sun off their heads. It looked almost like a fedora.

Who even wore fedoras? Gangsters? Spies?

They appeared deep in conversation.

Daisy tugged at the leash, eager to see her pal Nacho.

I had to dig my heels in to prevent her from pulling me over. She whined loudly.

"Easy, girl. I want to see where this is going."

I watched as the man talked animatedly at Aly, towering over her. He was tall and slender and dressed in what almost looked like army fatigues. *The kind of green clothing you would wear if you were trying to hide in the jungle.*

I couldn't hear anything. Aly was shaking her head. She turned to excuse herself, and the man grabbed her arm. She looked back, eyes wide, and wrenched her arm out of his grip. Nacho stepped in between her and the man.

At this point, Daisy had had enough. She continued to pull toward Nacho, looked back at me, and barked.

Three heads swiveled toward us.

The man looked at Nacho, glanced at me and Daisy, and turned on his heel, and walked quickly off into the jungle.

CHAPTER 16
THE MYSTERY OF C.M.

"Oh, I am so glad to see you," said Aly. She looked relieved. The two dogs began bouncing off each other in their canine meet and greet. Aly and I had to take a minute to untangle their leashes.

"Are you okay," I asked. "What was that all about?"

"Oh, that was nothing. Just a collector my parents know from the museum."

"It looked like he grabbed you."

"It was nothing," she said again.

Nothing. Sure looked like something to me.

"Right, well, I have something to show you. And I need your help. Tree house?"

"Sure," she said.

We walked to the treehouse in the gathering dark, Daisy, and Nacho leading the way. I found myself looking over my shoulder, spooked. But I figured the dogs would let us know if anything was after us.

Aly hooked Nacho into the rope at the bottom of the tree that she kept there for just that purpose. I did the same with Daisy. As long as she was with Nacho, she was happy as could be.

We climbed up into the tree house, and Aly lit the lamps. The height didn't bother me as much this time. She handed me a chocolate bar, which I accepted hungrily, having skipped most of my dinner.

"What is it?" she asked between chomps.

I opened my laptop. Being an older machine, the computer took some time blinking itself to life. I imagined a Yucatan squirrel in there running on a hamster wheel.

"Give me a second," I said as I hammered away at the keys and pointed this way and that on the track pad. I chewed my bottom lip as I searched.

Finally, I turned the screen toward her.

"Look what I found."

On the laptop was a picture of the dig site. Full screen, but pretty pixilated and lousy quality. It looked like something from one of the old TVs they have everywhere in Guatemala.

"Yeah," she said, glancing back up. "I was there."

Dad's laptop is filled with photos just like this. A bunch of lab techs scraping away at a big, dry rectangle of dirt. Sun beating down. Hard to tell who's who because they're always dressed very similarly and wearing big hats.

"Look in the upper-righthand corner."

She squinted her eyes at the screen. "Okay.." she said, not getting it.

"Here," I said, squeezing in next to her.

It was a little blurry, but I could make out two people, one taller than the other. They stood side to side, the taller one tilting his head down as if they were talking but wanted to be able to watch everyone else while they did so.

"Can't you see who that is?" I asked. I was getting tired of having to drag this along.

"Deacon," she said finally.

Sneakin' Deacon, I thought.

"So Deacon was talking to somebody at the dig site," I said. "And see the bulge in his backpack? It looks just like the shape of the statue. We just have to figure out who he was talking to." I pulled out the note with the numbers. "Then I found this note in his backpack today. It was written in code."

"It looks like a bunch of numbers to me. What does it say?"

"Meet me tonight at ten. River. C.M."

"Wow, how did you figure that out?"

"It's a Polybius Square Cipher," I said triumphantly. "We use them all the time in cryptography."

"Impressive," said Aly, smiling at me. "Let me see that photo again." She peered at the screen.

"I know him!" said Aly, excitedly bobbing her head. "That is Carlos Mortano. He owns the Maya River Tours."

I pushed a wet strand of hair back behind my ear. It was humid in the treehouse.

Carlos Mortano. Carlos Mortano. Carlos Mortano...

"C.M.!" I said, trying to keep from yelling. It was late, and I didn't want to draw any attention to us. "From the note!"

"Yes!" said Aly.

"Do you think that's who was with Deacon inside the Temple?"

Aly bit her lip and cocked her head. "Maybe."

"And the note I found today," I said, feeling my head buzz with excitement. "It said meet at the river..."

"Perhaps at the river tours boat house?" she said, looking at me with bright brown eyes.

I looked at my watch. It was 9:45.

"We only have fifteen minutes before they're supposed to meet," I said as I gathered my backpack. "Do you know how to get there?"

"Yes," she nodded. "And I even know a shortcut."

"Great," I said as we scrambled toward the tree house ladder. "Let's go."

We raced through the jungle after dropping off Daisy and Nacho at Aly's house.

Our flashlights created a little tunnel of light in the darkness. The jungle was an eerie black maze at this point, with only tiny pricks of moonlight breaking through. Aly's shortcut wound around the village and straight through the jungle to the river. I followed her lead.

As we ran toward the water, we discussed our options.

"I think we should just stay back and watch," said Aly, pausing to catch her breath.

"You don't think we should confront them?"

Okay, maybe I was looking for a second chance.

"It's too early. We don't really have any proof of anything. Just suspicions."

"I suppose you're right," I said. "But what if they have the statues?"

"I guess we will find out."

The river was more of a small creek than anything, but it was navigable by small craft. A few guides offered tours of the jungle in little speedboats, taking people to see some of the temples and a lot of the wildlife.

As if on cue, the howler monkeys began their evening song.

I shivered, despite the warm air.

I kept an eye on my watch, giving her updates as we ran.

Just as I huffed, "9:51," Aly stopped dead in her tracks. I ran smack into her.

"Aly, what are you—" the words caught in my throat. By the

light of the moon, I could see a vine moving, slowing in front of her. The jungle seemed practically woven out of vines, thick ones, skinny ones, long ones, short ones. They were everywhere.

But this didn't look like a vine...

It looked like a —

Snake.

And it was winding its way around her neck.

"Aly, don't move," I said, taking a cautious step forward.

It was fully wrapped around her now, like a slick scarf. It was about the length of my arm.

"Harley! Help!"

"Oh, no, oh no," I shouted, bouncing up and down.

This is it. This snake is going to squeeze Aly to death and I'm next.

She kept pulling at it, but every time I did so, it coiled a little tighter.

"Oh, I know, I know," I said and grabbed the tail of the snake and began to unwrap it. That seemed to work.

"Get it off! Get it off!" she yelled.

I slowly moved my hands up the body until I reached the head. Then it was loose enough that I could fling it away. The creature landed on the ground with a thud and quickly scampered back into the jungle.

"It was a baby boa," I said as we watched it go.

"If that is a baby, I would hate to meet its mama," she said, backing away from where it landed. "Thanks, Harley."

"No problem," I said.

Did I mention I don't like snakes? This didn't make me any fonder. But, when you've traveled all over the world to remote locations where very few humans live, snakes are always around. Luckily, Dad taught me a few tricks, like grabbing a boa by the tail.

I looked at my wrist and then grabbed Aly's.

"Come on. We have to go."

"What time is it?" she asked

"10:01," I whispered as we rounded a corner. She stopped suddenly, thrusting her arm in front of me.

"More snakes?" I croaked, dreading another encounter.

"No," Aly pointed up ahead. "We are here."

CHAPTER 17
HIDDEN IN PLAIN SIGHT

The river slithered through the dark night like a moonlit snake. I could see a series of small docks along the side and a small boathouse. Boats were tied up next to docks, bobbing up and down as the river flowed beneath them.

On a different day—one without a stolen statue, an impending apocalypse, and swirling clouds—I would have enjoyed a lazy cruise down the river.

But that was not the case today.

I studied the path of the water as it disappeared in the distance. Jessica had grilled me on my geography just last week. I knew from my map studies that the Rio Holmul wound its way through the jungle and down to Lake Petén Itzá.

I bit my lip.

It would be easy to sneak away from Tikal and climb out in Flores. The whole town sat on an island in the lake. Next stop the airport. And then the black market.

The perfect getaway for smuggling stolen artifacts.

Which only meant one thing.

Goodbye statues.

"I don't see them," Aly said, pushing aside a giant leaf.

I checked my watch for the hundredth time. It was 10:05 pm.

We squatted in some bushes just off the path about twenty feet from the docks. I looked around for more snakes, just in case. Or anything else that skittered or slithered or squirmed. We seemed okay.

No sign of the river captain or Deacon.

"Do you think we missed them?" Aly asked.

"I don't know."

Aly shook her head. "Maybe C.M. meant someone else."

"Let's give it a minute," I said.

My shirt was damp with sweat, and not just from the humidity.

If Dad checks my room, he's going to kill me. I'll be grounded until I leave for college.

I was about to give up and think of what I could do while I was locked in my room for the next six years when I saw a beam of light bouncing down the trail.

I tapped Aly on the shoulder. I put my finger to my lips and pointed.

Her eyes grew wide, and she sunk deeper into the bushes.

I did the same.

The light kept inching closer.

It passed right across Aly's head and swept towards my left arm. I snatched it out of the light, squeezing it back into the trees. The light seemed to hesitate, stopping right next to my foot.

But then it moved on.

A second later, I saw the brown boots of a certain British boy step about a foot from my face. Aly looked at me with a tight smile and a nod of her head.

I mouthed the words, "I knew it."

Just then, a curious little monkey dropped down from a nearby tree limb. He cooed and cackled and started to climb up my leg. I froze, afraid to swat him away.

Hopefully, monkeys didn't bite.

Deacon must have heard the little guy because he paused and looked over his shoulder. This time turning to scan the jungle, sweeping back and forth with his light. I tried to squeeze myself into the ground. The beam passed right over us and back down the trail.

I held my breath. The monkey left and suddenly scurried across the path, right in front of Deacon.

"Well, hello there," he said as he watched the monkey melt back into the jungle.

Then he started walking toward the docks again, his boots crunching on the path.

When he reached the docks, he stood there glancing up and down the river and then at his wrist. He had his backpack, which he put on the ground. It had the familiar lump in it, just like in the photos at the dig site.

He was far enough away from us to know that we could talk.

"Carlos is late," Aly said under her breath. "We made it right on time."

I nodded. "Deacon's backpack looks heavy."

Maybe heavy enough to have a statue inside.

The river's wavelets shone in the moonlight. But then I noticed another light playing across them.

"Someone's coming from downstream."

A boat was making its way toward the docks, navigating the current. I could see a figure paddling in the dark.

"He's not using his motor," I said. "Trying to go unnoticed."

"Suspicious," Aly replied with a nod.

The boat pulled up to the dock, rocking gently. The man onboard threw a line around a piling and held it there while Deacon climbed aboard. They talked a moment.

I leaned in to hear what they were saying, but the sounds of the howler monkey's song drowned out their voices.

Deacon opened his backpack and showed the man something inside. The man nodded and gestured for Deacon to sit down.

"Can you tell if that's Carlos?" I asked.

"Not from this far. But I would bet anything."

The boat pushed off from the docks. The man started paddling it out into the current.

"They are leaving!"

"I've got an idea," I said, jumping up and running as quietly as I could toward the water. "Come on!"

It only took seconds to get to the waterfront. Tied up to the docks were a couple of small Guatemalan canoes. I grabbed a couple of life jacket laying nearby and handed one to Aly.

"We have to follow them," I said.

"We cannot just take someone's boat!"

"If the three statues come together, it could be catastrophic for the world," I said, "and much worse than borrowing a boat. We'll bring it back."

Dad was going to kill me.

I put the life jacket on and stepped into the boat. We had to do something. And they were getting away.

Aly and I paddled furiously, trying to keep the other boat in sight. With the twists and turns of the river, it wasn't easy. But because the two of us were heaving at our oars, and only one person was paddling up ahead, we were gaining on them.

The moonlight dappled the surface of the river. After about five minutes, my arms felt like they were going to drop into the river.

"We don't want to get too close," I said, half out of breath.

"Right," said Aly. "Don't want them to see us."

Deacon was just sitting in the bow of his boat, looking at the jungle. He wasn't helping paddle at all.

The current was swift enough that it carried us along quickly. We didn't need to do too much to maintain our momentum. I imagined all the piranhas and water snakes in the black depths beneath me and shivered.

"It must be almost eleven o'clock," I said. "My dad and Jessica are going to be frantic wondering where I am."

"Just saving the universe," said Aly.

"I'm not sure they'll see it that way."

We kept pace with the other boat, hanging back about fifty yards, hoping they wouldn't notice us. About ten minutes passed and we continued to glide down the river. I looked back toward the village, worried we were getting too far away. When I pulled my eyes back toward the other boat, they were gone.

Where did they go?

"OMG!" said Aly suddenly, dropping her paddle into her lap and raising her hand to her mouth. "The falls."

"Umm, falls?"

"Yes, there is a 100-foot waterfall up ahead! We are headed right for it!"

CHAPTER 18

DANGEROUS FALLS

I could hear the thunder of the falls up ahead. There was no avoiding it. We were right in the middle of the river and the current was sweeping us directly toward it.

"Paddle hard right!" said Aly.

Even though my arms were aching, I dug hard into the water. We began to shift to the right side of the river. The sound of the falls kept getting louder as the current drew us closer. We had to get to the shore. I paddled harder.

We pulled, making a diagonal toward the jungle. The current pulled, dragging us closer to the lip. I paddled as hard as my exhausted arms would let me. The river was pushing us just as hard.

The falls were really roaring now. So loud we couldn't talk. The spray of the water blasted over the edge. Aly glanced back at me; her eyes as big as golf balls. All I could do was keep paddling.

Finally—finally!—we broke free of the current and entered the swirling eddy near the shore. I wanted to collapse with relief, but not until my feet were on solid ground.

"Made it," said Aly. "I was really worried there for a bit."

Worried was putting it mildly. I'd been terrified.

There were a series of wooden piers jutting into the water. Deacon and the guide had pulled into one, and the guide stood up, wrapping a line around a post. We aimed for one of the other docks, bending low in the boat to avoid being noticed.

No such luck.

"Aly? Harley? What are you two doing here at this hour?" Deacon stood on the dock above us. He shined his flashlight right down into our boat.

"Oh... um... uh... We decided to go out for a moonlight paddle," I said. "It's such a pretty evening."

"In my boat?" The river guide had joined Deacon on the dock. He pointed at the canoe we were still sitting in.

"Umm, about that.." said Aly.

We were busted.

Great.

My dad was going to lock me in my room forever. We tried to convince the river guide to let us go home, but he wasn't having it.

After a few minutes of pointless pleading and begging, he called our parents.

With our tails tucked between our legs, we were headed home.

∿

"HARLEY REBECCA JAMES, you are grounded. For the rest of the dig. You're not to leave the house without permission."

Dad was furious. I couldn't remember the last time he was so mad. When he got furious, his eyebrows did the cartoony thing where they made a big V.

They were making a big V.

It was the next morning, a gray, gloomy day, which was a surprise after the moonlit night. Clouds had rolled in after midnight, and rain was just waiting to pounce. Guatemala got heavy storms sometimes, which sucked all the moisture out of the jungle and spat it back down on top of everything. The rain was beginning to spit outside.

The lecture went about how I suspected: What did you think you were doing? Don't you know how dangerous the river is? And at night? What were you thinking about taking someone else's boat? How did you think you were going to get back home? Flores is not the kind of place for two twelve-year-old girls to be walking around at midnight.. On and on it went.

"Well, what do you have to say for yourself?"

I just looked at my feet. There wasn't much I could say. "Gee, Dad, we were trying to retrieve your statues and prevent the apocalypse."

Jessica paced around as we were talking, her head down, arms held tightly to her sides. I couldn't tell if she was angry or concerned. She'd been on the phone when we got back, which I thought was unusual so late at night. But she did have that boyfriend in the States. I don't know if they were breaking up or what, but she wasn't laughing or giggling like she normally did.

"You can go to your room. I don't even know what else to say."

I slunk back to my room, head down, the way Daisy does when she's been punished for eating food off the table. I left the door open a crack in case Daisy wanted to join me. She didn't like Dad yelling either.

Now, what? How was I going to get the statues if I was grounded?

They're probably halfway to Mexico City by now, anyway.

I pulled my backpack off the floor and slumped down on my bed. I rubbed the France patch with my thumb. It had a picture of the Eiffel tower in the center. I remembered the day Mom, Dad, and I had gone to see the most famous landmark in France. It was times like these I missed my mother the most. I was sure she would have all the right answers.

Okay, she would have been furious as well. Just because she knew what to say didn't mean she was a pushover.

After a few moments of feeling sorry for myself and the mess I had gotten into, I decided to see if I could reach out to Aly. I pulled my phone from my backpack and sent her a text message.

She had already messaged me.

"What now?" she wrote.

"We can't give up," I wrote back.

"I am grounded," she typed. "Stuck at home for the rest of my life."

"I'm grounded, too. But I'll think of something."

The wind was shaking the trees by my bedroom window, and it sounded like it was pouring, like the water over those falls. It seemed like Chac, the Mayan god of rain, was as angry as Dad.

After I heard Dad leave for work, I went to the kitchen to root about for something to eat. I was famished. Paddling desperately to avoid going over a waterfall sure worked up an appetite. My arms still ached.

I grabbed a cold enchilada from the fridge. Daisy looked at me like she wanted half. Those eyes. *If I could make those eyes, I probably wouldn't be grounded.* I broke off a chunk for her. Dad didn't like when I fed her table scraps, but I figured I was already in the doghouse.

"Harley."

I forgot Jessica was still here.

"Mmmmm?" My mouth was full.

"I need to go out to do something. I can trust you to stay home and finish your homework, right?"

"It looks pretty nasty out," I said.

Jessica nodded, pulling on her rain slicker, and tucking her hair into the hood. It was so bright yellow she looked like a duck.

"I'll be gone about an hour."

"Mmm hmmm," I said.

Jessica slid out the door, pulling it quietly shut behind her. Dad had taken the Jeep, so wherever she was going, she had to walk. I wondered why she hadn't gotten a ride with Dad.

And she forgot her umbrella. I grabbed it and figured I could score a few points if I ran it out to her. As I stepped to the door, I noticed something sticking out of the handle of the umbrella. It was a folded piece of paper.

Another note. What is with all these notes? I felt like a grade school teacher, intercepting secret messages.

It was a map, the kind they gave to all the tourists that visited Tikal. The visitor center must have a million of them. They were printed on slightly heavier paper than normal, which meant they were great for making paper airplanes.

Why would Jessica need a map? Why do tourists need these anymore? With smartphones?

I unfolded it on the table, nervously looking back at the door in case Jessica returned for her umbrella. Nothing was written on the backside. In the map's corner, near the Temple of the Grand Jaguar, an area of the jungle was circled with a red marker. Underneath was scribbled, "Estatuas. Uno."

Statues. One.

I stared at the note in my hand. This wouldn't be referring to *the* statue, would it? The one I had been chasing for the last few days?

CHAPTER 19

NOTHING IS AS IT SEEMS

A million thoughts went through my head. Was this Jessica's umbrella? How did that note get in there? Was she working with Deacon? She couldn't be. I'd spent nearly every waking moment with her for the past couple of months. She'd made me breakfast, lunch, and dinner. Nursed me back to health when I had the flu.

It couldn't be her. She was not behind this. But who was?

Not like I could figure out anything from my bedroom. But Dad would absolutely kill me if I left. He'd throw me into a water-filled cavern like the Mayans used to do with the young boys they sacrificed to the gods.

I sent a text over to Aly, but she wasn't responding.

I paced back and forth in the kitchen. There wasn't a lot of room for pacing, and I touched every inch of the floor. Daisy walked alongside me, looking up until she got tired of it and went over to her doggie bed and snuggled in.

I poked my head out the door to see if I could see Jessica. I looked both ways. Nobody was around. The rain had already stopped. It was like that in the jungle. The rain god Chac throws an ocean atop you, and then Kinich Ahau, the Mayan sun god, pushes him out of the way and smiles down.

When I opened the door, Daisy stood right up. It gave me an idea. Jessica said to finish my homework, but someone had to take care of the dog, right?

I sent another message to Aly.

Something's up. Found another note that Jessica dropped about the statues... Meeting out by the temple at one. I figure Daisy will need a walk, oh, about 12:30. Join me?

Seconds later, my phone beeped. It was Aly!

I'm in. I think Nacho will need a walk too at just about the same time

I sat down at the kitchen table with my homework. Somehow sixth-grade math had a hard time holding my attention.

Every time I read equations with Xs and Ys in them, I thought of the Mayan kings. Plus, I was never sure how algebra was going to help me in my life. Whatever was left of it after the Mayan apocalypse. All I kept thinking about was Jessica and Deacon and how they were involved. I'd never been a big fan of Deacon, but Jessica was someone I liked and trusted.

The hands on the clock couldn't move fast enough. Even Daisy seemed uptight. She'd lie in her bed, then get up and wander around, stand by the door, look at me, and walk back to her bed.

Finally, it hit noon. I snagged another snack from the fridge and gave Daisy some kibbles. The final twenty minutes seemed to last about two hours. When the minute hand finally clicked across the gap to 12:30, I stood up. Daisy did, too.

"Ready for a walk, girl?"

She wagged her tail and walked around me in a circle. I slipped her leash off the peg on the coat rack and clicked it onto her collar, still half expecting Jessica to walk through the door at any second. But she didn't. The coast was clear.

I stepped outside. The ground was still a little wet from the rain, and Daisy licked a muddy puddle. "Eeewww, Daisy, that's gross."

She didn't seem to mind.

I made it to Aly's place in record time. She was just opening the door for Nacho.

"Ready?" I asked.

"My mom just left," she said, smiling. "Ready when you are."

The meeting spot was deep in the jungle, no doubt for secrecy. Aly and I walked briskly, knowing we were both in huge trouble if we got caught. Dad would probably let me get away with taking Daisy out to do her business around the house. But he wouldn't be pleased to find I was exploring the jungle with Aly. Again.

The trees were alive with wildlife, which kept Daisy and Nacho entertained. They were swiveling their heads around like owls, looking at the lizards and birds.

Once we were out of the village, I showed Aly the map.

"Doesn't leave much room for interpretation, does it?" she said. "And Jessica had this?"

I explained how I found it and my theory that Jessica must be trying to get the statues back, too.

"You know, there is something I never told you about Jessica," Aly said, dodging a giant puddle as we walked.

"What's that?"

"Well, a few years ago, Jessica got into some trouble. She was working part time at the museum and a few pieces went missing. Mayan jewelry."

"Missing, as in stolen?"

"We thought so. Jessica was the only person who had access to the jewelry collection, other than my parents. But as soon as we called the police, the pieces reappeared in their original location."

"And you thought it was Jessica?"

"Yes, but since the jewelry was returned, we never pressed charges. She quit shortly after to continue her studies at school."

Suspicious, I thought. Very suspicious. Maybe I was wrong about Jessica after all.

My brain was dancing around this new revelation when Daisy suddenly jerked the leash from my hand.

"Daisy!" I said, reaching down to snatch it back up.

And then, I noticed the bushes waving in the same direction she was pulling.

This can't be coincidence.

"Come on, Aly," I said. "I think someone's following us."

We hurried toward the meeting spot.

We were almost there when we came around a corner and ran into Aly's mom. My breath caught in my throat. Mrs. Reyes managed the Villa rentals as well as the museum, so she was probably making her afternoon rounds.

"Aly? Harley? What are you two doing out here?"

Aly looked at her feet.

"Alejandra," Aly's mom continued, "You are supposed to be home, grounded."

All of a sudden, the jungle got quiet.

"We were just taking the dogs out, Mrs. Reyes," I said, jumping to my friend's defense. "Dogs need to walk; my dad always says."

"Well, they do," she agreed. "But they can be walked close to home and without friends. I am sure you are probably grounded too, Harley."

"Yes, ma'am."

"I don't know what has gotten into you two." She shook her head, disappointed. "We will have a long talk when we get home," she said, looking at Aly. "I will personally walk you back."

I opened my mouth to explain. It's always so awkward when your friends' parents get mad.

"Well, Mrs. Reyes—"

"We really thought the dogs should get out," said Aly quickly. "That is all."

Aly gave me one of those intense stares that said, "Keep your mouth shut." It was sort of the kids' version of the knowing look that Dad gave when the conversation turned to grown-up topics.

I nodded.

Mrs. Reyes started back the way we came. I felt like a prisoner of war on the way back. A soldier captured in the jungle. I need to get to Jessica. If she stole the statue, she would have to give it back. And she must know the legend is real.

We had just a few hours of daylight left before the thirteenth Baktun.

And I was moving in the wrong direction.

CHAPTER 20
AN UNEXPECTED ALLY

Mrs. Reyes led us through the jungle, moving briskly along the path, as if she were trying to continue her work out. I had to march double time just to keep up. At least she didn't say anything, so that was a relief. Not sure I could take another lecture.

The events of the last few days were bouncing around in my head like a hundred rubber balls. My mind first went to where it all started, the Mayan glyphs that caused the earthquake to rumble the ground and drop that little statue at my feet in the jungle. Then losing the statue. The cicadas, the lightning, the pink clouds... Deacon and his mysterious medallion. Jessica.

How did it all fit together?

And I knew we were nearing the final Baktun. A small opening of time where the Three Kings would return. That was less than twelve hours away. And things were getting weirder.

The Mayans were famous for their calendar. They were one of the first civilizations to keep track of time that way. According to the Mayan calendar, the world was supposed to end in 2012.

Obviously, that didn't happen.

But they did get a bunch right though, like the 365-day year that we still use today. Way ahead of their time.

I thought about the Legend of the Three Kings as drops of sweat popped up on my nose. And it wasn't from the heat.

Perhaps they were just off by a few years.

The walk back to the village seemed like an eternity. A knot of dread was twisting in my stomach. For sure Mrs. Reyes was going to tell Dad. I'd live out my last days carrying buckets of dirt around a dig site. Dad would never let me out of his sight again.

On several occasions, I could hear branches snapping in the jungle. Bird calls that almost sounded fake. I got that creepy feeling again that we were being followed.

That the jungle had eyes.

Maybe it was just the breeze. I assumed the deal had been done by now. What would be the point in following us? Overhead the clouds seemed to be gathering, the pink hue returning. I saw lightning in the distance.

That can't be good. Maybe Aly's brother was right about the zombies.

We were just a few hundred feet from the Villas when I saw a small figure standing in the middle of the path. It didn't seem to be moving. A glimmer of sunlight broke through the trees and a patch of red hair shimmered.

"Hello, Mrs. Reyes," Deacon said. "Nice to see you again. It's turned into a lovely day." He stood in the middle of the trail, a big crocodile grin on his pale face.

Deacon had effectively blocked our path. Mrs. Reyes had no choice but to stop.

"Hola, Deacon." She said. "I'm sorry we can't stop and chat today. I'm taking the girls home."

"I could walk Harley back for you," Deacon said, flashing

another grin. He glanced at me, Aly, Nacho, and Daisy. "Looks like you have your hands full."

Mrs. Reyes narrowed her eyes. "Would you see to it that she gets home and does not run off into the jungle?"

"It would be my pleasure," said Deacon, bowing slightly, like an actor at the final curtain. He was really giving her the British charm.

What was this about?

I raised my eyebrows at Aly. She shrugged. Her shoulders slumped, and she had her arms wrapped around her waist, holding onto her elbows. She looked defeated.

"Thank you, Deacon. That is a help. Alejandra and I have a lot to talk about."

Aly cringed at the words.

Deacon stepped aside, and Mrs. Reyes resumed her march; Aly, and Nacho trailing behind.

I was left with Deacon. We looked at each other. He smiled and reached down to pet Daisy, who wagged her tail.

Daisy, you traitor.

"Harley," he said. "I've been wanting to talk to you about something."

This was it. He was going to tell me he'd stolen the third statue and brought it to Carlos. That he'd completed his evil plan, and it was only a matter of time before the Three Kings were reunited for their death march. Then the earth would shutter, the skies would glow, and the Mayan apocalypse would begin.

But that wasn't what he said.

CHAPTER 21

S.M.A.L.L.

"I've been watching you," he started. "In the jungle. At the temple. On the river. And I've been impressed. You were able to decode my messages using the black light and the Polybius square cipher. Not to mention your performance in the JICC tournament—"

"How did you know—"

Deacon held up a hand, silencing me.

"At each turn, you were brave and made the right decisions," he continued.

I stared at him, my mouth hanging open like a giant fly trap.

If I made the right decisions, why was the world about to end?

"I think you could help us."

"Oh, no," I said. "If you've been watching me, you'd know I am one of the good guys. I have no interest in stealing artifacts."

"That's just my point."

Your point? I tilted my head at him.

"You see, Harley, I'm not here to steal artifacts and sell them. Or stop them from being displayed in a museum. I'm here to stop the Legend of the Three Kings from coming true."

My stomach did a somersault.

"You mean, you believe in the legend too?"

"I do," he wiped a piece of wet hair from his forehead. "Once all those strange things started happening—the pink clouds and the lightning—I knew we were in trouble. If the Three Kings are reunited on the eve of the thirteenth Baktun—"

"They could bring about the destruction of the world."

"Precisely." Deacon nodded, a flash of intensity crossing his eyes. "I thought I had it under control. I had one statue in my hands, but a man in army fatigues found me and chased me through the jungle. I dropped the statue trying to escape."

"I saw him!" I cried, cupping my hands to my mouth.

Deacon nodded. "He works for Professor Witherton. They've been trying to reunite the statues."

"And you're not?"

"No," he said, his eyes narrowing. "I'm a S.M.A.L.L. agent."

"Well, you're taller than me," I replied, slightly confused.

Deacon chuckled, a smile breaking across his freckled face.

"No, it's S-M-A-L-L. It stands for the Society of Mysterious Artifacts, Legends, and Lore."

He pulled the medallion from his shirt and thrust it towards my face, like a police detective at the front door. I leaned over to inspect.

It was the same medallion I'd found in the Temple of the Jaguar. A picture of an owl with a half-moon crown was engraved on the face and it was ringed by words. Society of Mystical Artifacts, Legends, and Lore.

"I found that in the Temple of the Jaguar."

Deacon shifted his stance. "I must have dropped it when I was running from the man in the temple. I saw you had it in your bag when we were on the zipline tour. So I slipped away after we had finished and retrieved it from your bag."

"You looked through my backpack! How dare you!"

I could feel a bit of heat rise in my cheeks.

"Well, if I remember right, Harley James, you did the same to me; otherwise, you wouldn't have found that note."

My shoulders relaxed. "I guess you're right."

"The medallion is important. You see, S.M.A.L. L is an ancient order that works to prevent the ancient powers of evil from returning to the world. Three Mayan Kings kinds of things. All of us are kids, most of whom, like me, have parents who travel a lot. We also have an interest in archeology and mythology. We are the good guys."

"No parents? Just kids?"

"We have a small council of adults who help us navigate some areas we can't control. But for the most part, yeah, we're all kids."

I cocked my head to the side. "Wait, if you're the good guys, then who are the bad guys?"

"There are way too many to name in this conversation. But in this case, I think we are working against an organization known as The Architects."

He tucked the medallion back into his khaki-colored shirt. I watched him and shifted the weight of my backpack. The heat from the jungle was sapping away my energy. But I was intrigued.

Was he really a secret agent?

"They pose as architects because it allows them to visit temples and other structures where valuable artifacts are kept. They just pretend they're studying buildings. But they are really the Architects Advancing the Apocalypse, or Triple-A, a secret society dating back to before the pyramids."

"Are they like the Illuminati?" I asked. Dad had always been fascinated by the Illuminati, a secret society of world leaders.

"Sort of, I guess," Deacon said. "Just trying to bring about the world's downfall."

"What's in it for them?"

"Control. They believe if they can harness the power of the Mayan Kings, they can rule the world. They believe it would give them unlimited power."

"Wow."

Makes sense, I guess.

I fumbled with the straps on my backpack. It was a lot to take in.

"Our motto is to preserve, protect and persevere. The three P's."

He flipped over the medallion to show me the engraving on the back. I could see the three P's as well as the words he described.

"We've been watching you for some time. And we think you'd be an ideal agent," Deacon said. "We want you to join us."

Wait, what? Me join some secret organization of kid spies? I leaned on a nearby tree trunk. I was not agent material. Here I thought Deacon was the bad guy? I hadn't really proved myself as far as I could see.

"Me, an agent? I'm just a kid."

"Haven't you been listening? We're *all* just kids. You'd be amazed what kids can do. We've stopped the Architects again and again." Deacon brushed a hand through his orange hair. I squinted at him in the sunlight, trying to process all this new information.

"Have you heard of the Timur Curse? Or the Bjorketorp Rune?"

I shook my head.

"No, you haven't because we were able to stop them. And we're going to stop this threat too. We're going to get back those statues. We have to before they fall into the wrong hands."

"I agree with you there," I said, standing up. Even if I didn't completely trust Deacon or believe all this stuff about some secret kid spy organization, at least we seemed to want the same thing at the moment.

Just then, a clap of thunder echoed in the distance. Deacon and I turned our heads in unison. It was all happening again, this time at once. The pink clouds were getting darker, and cicadas started their song as if on cue.

"I think it's time we go," said Deacon, looking back at me. "How well do you know your Mayan glyphs?"

I shrugged. "Pretty well."

"Then follow me. We have another riddle to solve. And I'm going to need your help."

And with that, Deacon turned from me and headed back down the path.

CHAPTER 22
WHICH WAY DO WE GO?

Daisy bolted after Deacon. I had no choice to follow.

Deacon a good guy? Me, a secret agent? Ancient secret societies?

It was a lot to process. My mind spun as I pounded up the trail after them. Whatever he was, Deacon was fast. He and Daisy were already several yards ahead of me. I sprinted as fast as I could, stretching my legs forward like they were made of taffy.

Deacon took a sharp right turn into the jungle, and I followed. But just as I rounded the corner, he had sputtered to a stop. Rising up through the jungle was a massive temple. It was larger than the Temple of the Jaguar. And we were a long way from Tikal.

"What is this place?" I said, catching my breath.

"El Templo Escondido," said Deacon, walking back to stand next to me. "The Hidden Temple."

"Wow," I said. It towered above the trees, nearly two hundred feet high. Like the other temples, it had terraces that wrapped up the sides and large stones steps that cascade down the front. But there was something special about this temple. It was painted. Rich reds, vibrant greens, and yellows wound up and down the sides of the building. All the colors fit together perfectly, like a Mayan game of Tetris.

"Ready for a hike?"

I gulped. I had already been at the top of one of these temples. I wasn't exactly excited about the idea of climbing down from another. But there was a lot at stake.

"Lead the way," I said, gesturing towards the top.

I held on to Daisy's leash tightly, and we followed Deacon up the side of the temple. We huffed and puffed up at least a hundred steps. My legs were aching as we marched. Sweat was running down my back like a tiny river. I kept my eyes focused on each step in front of me rather than look up or down.

I could hear my mother's voice in my head suddenly.

One step at a time, honey.

"We're here," I heard Deacon say as I finished a final couple of steps.

I looked up, and my jaw dropped.

The structure in front of us was even more beautiful up close. In addition to the carved stones, there were rows and rows of paintings. I could see people growing corn, worshiping their Gods, and the Gods themselves fighting each other. It was like staring at the Mayan version of a comic strip. Only instead of jokes and cartoons, there were human sacrifices.

Gross.

Anyway, in the center was a tall doorway that seemed to lead inside the temple.

"This is incredible," I said, waving my hand towards the paintings.

"It's great, but we need to move," Deacon said, taking several long strides towards the doorway. The strange clouds gathering over the temple seemed to be getting darker. "This way."

We stepped inside. A long hallway stretched out before us, peppered with torches that were glowing in the dark. I kept close to Deacon as we charged ahead. We were moving so quickly I didn't even have time to reach for the headlamp in my backpack.

Daisy was panting by my side as we stepped into the low light. At the end of the hall, we stumbled upon a set of stone steps that led down deeper into the temple. Despite my determination to find those statues, I hesitated.

"Are you sure this is safe?"

Deacon glanced over his shoulder. "I'm sure. I came down here before. I know the way."

"Then why do you need my help?"

"You'll see," he said as he skipped down the steps.

We had just climbed up a hundred feet and now it seemed we were climbing back down.

Apparently, the Mayan's did not believe in shortcuts.

When we reached the bottom, the narrow stairway gave way to another long hallway. We walked for about thirty feet before arriving in a large circular cavern. It smelled musty, like the old moldy tent Dad and I used one summer at a dig site in Nevada.

The ceilings towered above us, nearly ten feet high. More torches flickered against the wall, revealing elaborate stonework, paintings, and several doorways. Centipedes, spiders, and other bugs I didn't recognize crawled around on the floor. *Eww!*

All the doorways looked exactly the same. In fact, as we walked toward the center of the room, I realized I had no idea which way we came in.

"How many—"

"There are nine," Deacon said, interrupting my thoughts. "Nine doorways."

Of course. The Nine Levels of the Underworld.

"Which one do we take?"

Deacon looked at me, his green eyes catching the light. "That's where you come in, Harley James. I need you to tell me."

I stared back at him. "How would I know?"

I took a deep breath. *Pull it together, Harley.* If the exit was written in code, where would I begin?

Deacon walked over to one of the torches and pulled it from the wall. He raised it close enough to the top of one of the openings.

"Do you see those?"

Above the doorway, I could see several painted stones. Each was carved with a symbol.

"Mayan glyphs," I whispered.

"Right, I believe one of these leads to a ceremonial location inside the temple grounds. That's where they've taken the statues. We need to get there before they are reunited. But I don't know which door to take."

I grabbed a torch from the wall and began to search around the room. Daisy stayed close to my feet as we marched from one to another. Each doorway had six glyphs above it. After a while, I noticed a pattern... and I recognized the glyphs.

"I've seen these before."

"Where?" said Deacon, spinning around to look at me from his corner of the room.

"In the jungle, when I found the first statue."

"You had one of the statues?"

"Yes, I was going to give it to Dad, and then someone stole it from my room."

"Right, bloody bad luck."

It wasn't luck, I thought. Stolen was more like it.

"There were six Mayan glyphs," I said, my eyes scanning the room. "Jaguar, Sun, Snake, Rain, Skull, and Earth. And they were placed in that order. If we can find the doorway with the same order, then that's the one we follow."

Deacon and I stood back to back as we peered around the room. "There!"

We both rushed forward to the same doorway. All the symbols were there, in the same order as they had been in the jungle. *Jaguar, Sun, Snake, Rain, Skull, and Earth.*

Deacon turned to face me. "Ladies, first," he said, gesturing towards the opening.

I sure hoped I was right.

After a few minutes of walking, I could see a tiny pinprick of light in the distance. My heart skipped a few beats faster. It was sunlight. We were heading back outside.

"Look," I said, pointing ahead.

"You did it, Harley! Bloody brilliant!"

I blushed. It wasn't often I received such high compliments for my solving puzzles. Mostly just smiley face emojis on the internet. Deacon was starting to grow on me.

"Thanks," I said, tightening my grip on Daisy's leash. "Let's go."

A few minutes later, we stepped back out into the heat of the jungle. I was momentarily blinded by the sunlight. I raised my hand to block the sun, trying to get my bearings.

Daisy started barking. She yanked the leash from my hand and darted away from me.

I knew that bark. It was one she saved for greeting people she knew.

CHAPTER 23
A TRAITOR AMONGST US

"Daisy!" I cried as my eyes adjusted to the sunlight. We had just stumbled into a square clearing inside the temple grounds. Rising up all around us were towering walls. I quickly scanned the area. It seemed there was only one way in or out, and that was through the door we just escaped through.

When I saw what was in the middle of the clearing, I stopped dead in my tracks.

There was a large altar, with about a dozen steps leading to the top. A large stone slab covered the surface with three squares stones rising on the top. I could see two green glowing statues resting in place.

Above that was a swirling pink and green cloud that stretched into the sky. The wind kicked out from this cyclone and whirred around the clearing. The sound of the wind was so loud I could barely hear myself think. And the cicadas, they were here too.

The ground rumbled beneath my feet.

Uh oh, that's not good.

I watched as Daisy ran straight ahead to Jessica. I recognized her long legs and carefully braided hair from a mile away. The satchel she carried everywhere was hanging from her shoulder. In her hand was something glowing...

She has the statue.

Standing across from her at the altar was a group of men I didn't recognize. They seemed to be involved in a heated conversation.

Wait, a second...

I did recognize one of them; the man in the army fatigues! And he seemed to have brought some friends; two of them, in matching outfits.

This can't be good.

The last man of the little group at the altar was dressed completely differently. He was wearing a khaki linen suit with a matching hat that had a red sash wrapped around it. He seemed to be in charge. As soon he saw us, he started waving his hands in our direction.

"Professor Witherton," I heard Deacon whisper as he caught up with me. He touched my arm and whispered, "We have to be careful."

Every bone in my body was screaming for me to run in the other direction. But I stood my ground. Daisy had already crossed the distance between us and the altar.

The wind was blowing so hard it nearly knocked me over. I took a few steps forward.

"Daisy," Jessica said, bending down to greet her, "What are you doing—" she jerked her head up to look around. That's when she saw me.

The next few moments went by in a flash. Deacon was suddenly in front of me, running towards Jessica. She tucked the statue under her arm and bounded up the steps. She was just about to the top, when Deacon leaped forward and grabbed the satchel hanging from her shoulder.

Jessica was suddenly thrown off balance. She faltered on the top step and nearly tumbled down the side of the altar. She extended her arm out to catch herself, but, in doing so, lost control of the statue. It fell from her hands and bounced off the step below her.

The statue!

Deacon stretched his arms out to catch it as it arced through the air, but his back foot slipped on the altar steps. He landed face-first on hard stone and cried out in pain.

"Deacon!" I yelled.

The statue kept tumbling down the steps like a slinky toy.

The men in fatigues didn't hesitate, they were making their way around the side of the alter. I could hear the professor shouting, but I couldn't understand his words.

I had an advantage. I was much closer to the statue than anyone else.

I ran with all the energy I had left to reach the statue. I scooped it up with both hands. It seemed to be pulsing with a green light inside and vibrating in my hands.

Jessica ran toward me, the army men right on her heels.

"Harley! What are you doing here?"

She was just a few feet away. I started taking a few steps back toward the temple. "Stop right there, Jessica; don't come any closer."

"Give me the statue back, Harley. This doesn't concern you."

"Concern me? These statues are dangerous! Haven't you heard the legend?"

"The Legend of the Three Kings is a fairytale for children. It's not real."

"Open your eyes, Jessica, and look around you! Do you not see the glowing statues, the clouds, hear the cicadas?"

"We get crazy weather all the time here in Guatemala."

I could see there was no point in arguing with her.

"This doesn't belong to you, Jessica. It belongs in a museum. I'm here to protect it."

Jessica snorted. "Oh really, is that why you had one of the statues tucked under your bed?"

She stood facing me with her hands on her hips. The two men in army fatigues were standing behind her, glaring at me. "Just give me a minute," she said, glancing back at them.

"I was going to give them to Dad," I replied. "I wasn't keeping them for myself."

"Right," she said. "Well, it doesn't matter now. Give me the statue."

I took a step back, my confidence slipping. Daisy ran over to my side.

"No way."

"Harley, don't make this harder than it has to be."

"I can't. This belongs to the Tikal Museum. The Flores family, they will keep it—"

"Keep it, what, Harley? Safe?" She let out a puff of air. She used to do that sometimes when she was frustrated with my schoolwork. "Keep them locked in a tiny museum where no one will see them? I don't see the point. My buyer will take them to the largest museum in Europe. The Three Kings of the Maya—millions of people will learn their story." She narrowed her eyes. "And I will make enough money to fund my own research."

She took a step toward me. "It's a win-win for everyone. Now give me the statue, Harley."

Just as I was about to crumble under pressure, I heard a voice off to my left.

"Hey, over here!"

Everyone looked. It was Deacon. He was running back up the altar to make a grab for the other two statues. It gave me just enough time.

I turned back towards the temple doorway and ran.

CHAPTER 24
THE REAL LEGEND

A few months ago, I had this dream that I was flying. I jumped from building to building, bouncing through the sky. That's how I felt as I sprinted back towards the temple—like I was flying. My feet were moving so fast they barely touched the ground.

Daisy had joined me in my sprint for the temple entrance. Apparently, I was much more interesting right now than Jessica. I tried not to look behind me, but I was sure that Jessica would be hot on my heels in no time. I still had the glowing statue tucked under my arm.

I had to find a place to hide. Or get back outside into the jungle. After a few minutes, I skidded to a stop. I was back inside the circular room of doors. Just like before, as soon as I entered and turned around, I wasn't sure which was the way out.

The torches were still flickering against the walls, giving out just enough light so I could see the Mayan glyphs illuminated in the darkness. I scanned the room and quickly spotted the doorway from which I came.

I was definitely not going back that way.

What I needed to know now was which doorway led to the stairs. Okay, so let's think. All the symbols above the doors are the same: Jaguar, Sun, Snake, Rain, Skull, and Earth. By matching the order of the symbols to the stone wall I found in the jungle, we found our way to the altar.

In the rest of the doorways, the symbols were mixed in random orders that made little sense. Were they all meant to just point to the exit? Surely not. Or did they lead to other places in the temple? I only wanted to find the stairs.

Think, Harley!

Okay, if that was the order that brought me outside, then perhaps the reverse order would take me the other direction.

Daisy was yipping at my feet as I turned around in the room. "Shh, girl, I'm trying to think."

Then I spotted it. Earth, Skull, Rain, Snake, Sun, and Jaguar! The symbols are in reverse!

"Harley! Come back here," I heard Jessica's voice echo in the distance.

Now or never.

I bolted toward the doorway; Daisy glued to my side. It was darkness for a few steps, and I started to second guess my decision. But just as I was about to turn back, my foot caught on the first step, and I stumbled forward. The statue slipped out of my hands.

"No!" I said, lunging forward. I landed on the steps with a thud. The statue landed back in my hands. Whew, that was close.

This time, I tucked the statue in my backpack. "Let's go, Daisy!"

We bounded up the stairs, two at a time. I have never climbed so many stairs in my life! My shirt was soaked all the way through. I could feel the steps slick with moss under my feet, but I somehow kept my balance. The musty smell was growing weaker, so I knew we must be getting close to the top.

I could hear noises and shouting somewhere below me, but I pushed ahead. When I reached the top of the stairs, I finally had to stop and catch my breath. My lungs felt as if they had caught fire and were burning a hole through my chest.

After a few moments, we headed towards the temple exit. I could see the sunlight piercing through the clouds ahead and a thumping noise in the distance. I ran outside and looked up. Flying overhead was a helicopter, its rotating blades flattening the treetops as it swung over the jungle. I squinted my eyes. I could see the outline of a khaki hat with a red sash sitting in the dashboard of the cockpit.

I guess Professor Witherton had decided to make a grand exit.

As I stood there staring for a moment at the sky, I realized there were no more swirling clouds. The ground wasn't shaking...the cicadas had stopped singing.

We did it!

My sense of relief was cut short when I heard a voice creep up behind me.

"Harley!"

I whirled around to see Jessica standing at the temple entrance. She had finally caught up with me. She was slick with sweat and panting heavily. She walked toward me.

"Statue, now," she said. Her face was pinched. I had never seen her so angry. Daisy began barking at her, and she edged closer to me.

I looked to my left and right. There were only two ways down the temple. One, I could try to run down the moss-covered steps. But they were steep, and I was afraid I might fall.

The second option? There were two large channels that ran down the sides of the temple steps, basically, like two big waterslides, minus the water. It gave me an idea.

"It's never gonna happen," I said as I backed up toward the edge of the temple terrace.

"If you try to make it down those steps, you'll fall. Give me the statue, and we can go down together."

She reached out to pull the statue from my arms. Just a few more steps....

Here goes nothing!

I turned on my heel and jumped on the stone channel. It was like a waterslide, all right! I zipped down the edge of the temple like a bobsledder in the Olympics.

"Whooaaa..... Ahhhh!"

The jungle floor was coming sooner than I would have liked. I could see some grass and bushes rushing up to meet my feet.

Thud. I landed on the ground. I looked over my body. No broken bones, I could see. I jumped to my feet and looked back up. Jessica was standing at the top of the temple, still yelling my name.

"Harley, are you okay?"

I twirled around to the familiar voice.

"Dad!"

I was so relieved I nearly broke down and cried then and there. Dad was standing in the jungle, in his field clothes, holding his arms out to me. He ran to where I was standing and checked me over.

"You look alright," he said, running his hands over my arms. "Does anything hurt?"

"No, no. I think I'm okay. How did you find me?"

"The boy, Deacon. He sent his mother a text message. He said to come here to the Hidden Temple. That you were in trouble."

"Oh," I said. I looked back up at the temple. Jessica was gone. Daisy was carefully walking down the steps one at a time.

"Deacon is still inside. He might need help."

"It's okay. His mother is on her way in to find him. There is another entrance on the other side of the temple."

Oh, that would have been helpful to know.

I pulled my backpack off my shoulders and reached inside. "Look, I found the statue. One of the three Mayan kings."

"Wow," he said, his eyes twinkling with excitement. He turned it over in his hands. "But where did you get this from?"

"It's a long story," I said. "And, Dad, Jessica is not who you thought she was."

Dad pushed some hair from his face and gave me a serious look. "I know, Harley. You know the missing pieces of jewelry from the Tikal Museum? We found them in her room."

"You did?"

"Yes, the police should be arresting her soon."

"Oh, wow."

Dad nodded. "Let's head home. And while we're walking, you can tell me all about how you found this statue."

I smiled. I'm not sure he's ready for that story.

"Sure. But first, I need a drink of water."

CHAPTER 25
BACK WHERE WE BELONG

"Harley, I'd like you to help me with something." Dad peeked his head inside the door. Even after I explained everything, I was still grounded. Rules were rules. Even when you save the world.

I was reading on the couch with Daisy. Or, I should say, I was trying to read. It was hard to concentrate. So much had happened, and I was still processing it all. I always liked Jessica. And, of course, she brought me Daisy. But talk about someone keeping secrets and lying. It was still hard to believe.

After spotting Dad, Jessica had run off into the jungle—right into Aly and her brother Ricardo, who stopped her and turned her into the authorities. When they heard the news, Aly's mom let her join her brother in the search. She probably could have overpowered them, but by that point, she'd given up. They knew about the stolen jewelry, and it was only a matter of time before she was arrested.

"Come on, girl," I said. Maybe I could give Daisy a walk while I helped Dad. I put my book down and uncurled myself from the cushions. At least it was a chance to get out of the house.

We walked up the road.

"I've been thinking about it more, and I'm really proud of you, Harley. That was some scary stuff—and some clever thinking. You know what I always say. What the world needs now is people who know how to solve problems."

I smiled. "Thanks."

"I still don't know how you knew the correct order of the Mayan glyphs," he said, giving me a sideways smile. I had told him *most* of the story. How I found the statue in the jungle and how Jessica stole it from my room. But might have left out a few things, like how I found the statue in the first place.

"Just lucky, I guess."

"Hmmm," he said. Before I knew it, we were at the Tikal Museum.

"Well, we're here." He held the door for me and waved me in.

The first person I saw was Deacon. He was looking at a scale model of the Temple of the Grand Jaguar in one of the display cases.

"Deacon!" I said, running over to greet him. "I'm so glad you're alright!"

It was the first time I'd seen him since the debacle at the Hidden Temple. He leaned down to pet Daisy, who gave him a lick on the cheek.

"Harley! Same to you," Deacon replied. He stood back up to face me. "Thanks for all your help."

"Me? It was nothing," I blushed for a moment. "Thanks for calling in my Dad. I was so happy to see him waiting outside the temple."

He smiled and shrugged.

Dad was waiting for me across the lobby. "Harley, I wanted you to be part of this. You did all the hard work." He paused. "You too, Deacon."

He walked us to his office and pointed to the satchel, which sat on the desk.

"Look inside."

I peered in. Two of the three statues of the kings were there. As well as a bunch of smaller artifacts.

"How did you get one of the other statues?"

"It was Deacon," Dad said, nodding towards him. "He found it at the Hidden Temple."

I looked over at Deacon, who gave me a sheepish smile.

I was happy to see that they weren't glowing or flashing or making the ground shake. But the time of the thirteenth Baktun had come and gone.

"Wow," I said.

"Don't wow me," Dad said. "You two saved these. I wanted you to be the ones to place them in the new exhibit, 'The Lost Kings of the Maya.'" He paused, his hand on the desk. "We're still not sure what happened to the third statue. When Jessica was arrested, she said she had all three. If that one ever surfaces..." he trailed off, gazing out the window at the jungle.

Deacon and I exchanged a look. We knew exactly what happened to the third statue. *Professor Witherton*. It was probably in a secret vault somewhere, where the Architects kept all their stolen booty.

The three of us spent several hours helping to ready the new exhibit. We put the statues in locked see-through cases and set them on pedestals. A restoration expert had cleaned and polished them so that they glowed in the light. A different, safer sort of glow, not a destroy-the-world kind of glow.

From atop their stands, the statues faced toward the temple. Proud kings who could be honored without being dangerous.

When we finished, Deacon asked, "Harley, can I walk you home?" And my dad nodded his agreement.

"Sure," I said.

Deacon held the door as I stepped out into the sun. Daisy was happy to see us. After being in the dark museum, it took a minute for my eyes to adjust to the brightness.

"I have something to talk to you about."

As we strolled through the village, he told me that he was serious about me joining S.M.A.L.L.

"Harley, the talents you've shown," Deacon said, shaking his head. "Some of our agents would have had a difficult time handling this mission. Your cryptology skills. All that high angle stuff..."

"High angle?"

"Hanging off cliffs and climbing up steep pyramids and... Well... A lot of people are afraid of heights."

That made me smile.

"Will you consider it?"

"I will. But I might need a little break before the next adventure."

"A break?" he chuckled. "I understand. Still, you'd make a great field agent."

He looked down at his feet, disappointed. Daisy glanced at him and then at me, giving us a slight wag of her tail.

"Well, I'm still considering all my options."

"Can I send you some information? It would be by secret courier."

Secret courier? Now that sounded intriguing.

"Sure. I'd be happy to take a look."

By that time, we'd reached my front door.

"Goodbye, Harley. I hope you'll join us," Deacon said, extending his hand. I shook it.

He brushed his hair out of his face and smiled. He knelt down to dog-level. "Goodbye, Daisy. I hope you'll join us too."

She gave him one of her trademark open-mouth dog grins and wagged her tail.

"Goodbye, Deacon," I said, turning to walk in. "Thank you."

CHAPTER 26
TO NEW ADVENTURES

As I sat and waited for Dad to return, I pulled my knees up to my chest on the couch. I had such a lump in my throat that it felt like I'd swallowed a whole apple. Daisy hopped up and sat next to me. I patted her head. With Jessica gone... I looked over at Daisy.

"I don't want to go anywhere without you," I said.

She licked my nose and nuzzled my chin. Then she looked at me with big sad dog eyes. *Nothing is worse than sad dog eyes.*

I wrapped my arms around her neck and buried my face in her fur.

Just then, the door opened, and Dad walked in. He saw my red eyes and the way I was hanging on Daisy.

He sat on the couch next to us. Daisy tilted her head toward him.

"Well, Cat-Cat, I have some good news and some bad news," he started.

"Might as well give me the bad news," I said, feeling sorry for myself.

"Jessica will be serving time for her role in the theft of the jewelry from the museum and the artifacts. Guatemala has strict laws about stealing artifacts and other national treasures. This took me all very much by surprise. I thought she was a fine tutor."

I nodded. I could see where this was going.

"As for Daisy..." he said, looking me in the eyes. I could feel the tears climbing out onto my eyelids.

"Wait—" he said, holding up his hand. "Guatemala already has enough waterfalls. The judge in the case has placed Daisy into our care. Obviously, Jessica won't be able to care for her. Jessica asked for this herself."

The tears broke free.

Dad sat up straight, confused. "I thought this was good news."

"It is," I sniffled. "These are tears of relief."

Daisy began to lick them off my face.

And that's how it went.

~

A FEW DAYS LATER, there was a knock on the door. I opened it to find Aly standing there.

"Hey," she said.

"Hey," I replied, waving her inside.

"Is your dad around?"

"No, he's at the museum."

"Then I have something for you," she said, reaching into her pack. Inside was a package, a box about the size of a laptop. Aly handed it to me. It had no address, but an owl with a half-moon crown was stamped in one of the corners.

I held it in my hands and stared at her.

"You're S.M.A.L.L.?"

"I like to think of myself as average height," she said, smiling.

Then she nodded. "I am so sorry; Deacon wouldn't let me tell you. He did not think it was time, and he wanted to see what you could do. I really wanted to." She pointed at the package. "Open it."

I tugged at one of the corners. It was one of those mailing boxes held together with super glue. I pulled and pulled.

"Some agent," Aly said, laughing. "Here," she pointed at the little perforated strip made for easy opening.

I grabbed the tag and dragged it back. Then I reached in, pulling out a folder with paperwork. A manual of some kind. And a medallion.

It was just like the one Deacon wore. Engraved on the front was the owl logo with the Society of Mysterious Artifacts Legends and Lore circled around it. I flipped it over to see the motto on the back with the three P's.

I ran my fingers over the words. *Preserve. Protect. Persevere.*

It looked like he had made the offer official. For some reason, I thought of my mother. I knew she would be proud of me for everything I had done while I was here. Facing my fears, doing what was right.

And she did have an affinity for myths and legends...

Just then, Dad opened the front door. "What's this?" he asked, taking off his jacket.

"Nothing," I said. "Just hanging out with Aly."

"Hmmm."

He walked into the kitchen, turning in the doorway.

"Hey," he said. "I just got some great news. I've been offered a job at one of the most well-preserved archeological sites in the Western hemisphere."

"Oh, really? And where is that?"

"The sunken pirate city of Port Royal, Jamaica."

My mind flooded with visions of pirates, treasure hunts and, of course, white sand beaches.

"When do we leave?"

ABOUT THE AUTHOR

Leah Cupps is an author, designer, entrepreneur, and self-proclaimed bookworm. She conceptualized the Harley James series with her oldest daughter, Savannah, who had developed an interest in Mayan history.

The mother & daughter duo worked together to create a new world, which became the foundation for the first Harley James series.

Leah resides in Indiana with her husband and three children. She is also the co-founder of the small family-owned publishing company Vision Forty Press.

Did you like this book and want to help spread the word?

It would mean a lot to me if you would leave a short review online. Every review helps with visibility and allows me to write more books.

Thank you,
Leah Cupps

READY FOR THE NEXT ADVENTURE TO BEGIN?

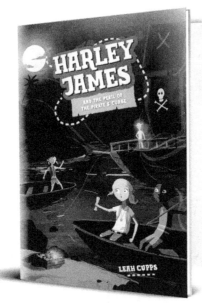

Book 2: Harley James & the Peril of the Pirates Curse

Join Harley and her friends as they swashbuckle their way through the mysteries of Port Royal, Jamaica—the famouse sunken pirate city of the Carribbean!

ORDER NOW AT AMAZON.COM

Book 3: Harley James & the Secret of the Falcon Queen

Harley and her friends race against time to keep the Queen's secret... a secret that has been kept for a thousand years in a mysterious castle in Scotland.

ORDER NOW AT AMAZON.COM

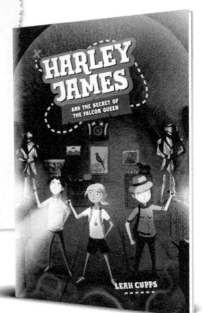

Made in the USA
Middletown, DE
23 October 2022